Dry Land Sailor

Front jacket illustrations:

The author (left) with “Skipper” John Knill
aboard Columba and Uranus at
Sampson Road Depot, Birmingham, 1949.

The flowers, from the back cabin of the butty Raymond,
are by the last of the great dock painters, Ron Hough.

Dry Land Sailor

Fred Hobbs

Foreword and
edited by
Geoffrey Lewis

SGM
Publishing

ISBN 978-0-9545624-9-6

Printed and bound in the UK by
MPG Biddles Limited, King's Lynn, Norfolk

First published in Great Britain in 2009 by

SGM Publishing

SGM Publishing
35 Stacey Avenue, Wolverton, Milton Keynes, Bucks MK12 5DN
info@sgmpublishing.co.uk
www.sgmpublishing.co.uk

For all boat men and women
of past and present

Foreword

I have been attending, and enjoying, the excellent canal festival at Linslade for a number of years now, and it was there that I met Fred Hobbs. I was sitting beside my own boat, the Elkhound, with a little table, signing copies of *Boy Off The Bank,* when this pleasant, grey-haired gentleman came up; we began to talk, and he introduced himself. When he told me he had worked on the boats in the years after the Second World War, my ears pricked up, and we carried on chatting for some time. It was during the course of this conversation that he first told me that he had actually written down his reminiscences of those days – but the manuscript was with someone else, who had promised to type it out for him. He did say that he would send me a copy of the finished article, when it arrived.

A year went by – the manuscript never arrived, and to be fair I forgot all about it. Then the next Linslade Festival came around; there I was again, this time with *Girl At The Tiller* added to my repertoire. Now I was sitting next to the Raymond, having sold my boat and since become the captain for the Friends of Raymond, who own and run that historic boat along with the Nutfield, its motor from the days of Blue Line. Along came Fred again; once more we got chatting, and I remembered that manuscript. It was, it transpired, still in the hands of the other typist, but Fred offered to get it back, in whatever form, and send it to me. I was keen to see it, partly because his story covered the exact period of the canal trade that I was writing about, but mostly because I had by now learnt that he had worked alongside some names that we all now hold in great esteem – the likes of Bill Humphries and Jack Skinner (Joe's nephew), Jack Munk, and even the man he called 'Skipper': John, later to be *Sir* John, Knill.

And when the manuscript turned up, a couple of months later, still hand-written, I settled down to read it. It is a fascinating story – Fred's boating career took the form of a series of relatively short incarnations, but that very fact is what introduces us to so many of the great characters of the time, and the picture he paints of the job and the way of life as well as the people held me enthralled. This is a trade, a way of life that is gone forever – and it will be forgotten, along with the skills that were a part of it, unless people like Fred are prepared to tell their stories before it is too late.

I have been delighted to act as editor for this published version of his memoirs, to be able to contribute in some small way to seeing it made available for others to read; and to pen this brief foreword to introduce his tales has been a rare privilege for me.

Geoffrey Lewis
March 2009

Preface

This book is the story of my own personal experiences of working on the boats, on the Grand Union and other canals. It has been my wish for many years to share those memories with others, especially those who holiday on our waterways and the dedicated people who strive to keep this part of our heritage alive for its original purpose.

I first worked on the boats with Bill and Iris Humphries, who took me on as a rank newcomer in late 1948; after various experiences I joined the army in 1951, only returning to civvy street in 1954. A chance meeting with Jack Monk saw me back on the boats again, and I remained 'on the cut' until late in 1956 when I went back to living on the bank. During those periods I was privileged to meet, and in many cases work with, some of the finest people I have ever known, and I have to thank them all for their readiness to accept, and their patience with, a non-boater such as myself.

And so it is that I would dedicate this book to all boat men and women of past and present, and to those who, also in times past and present, have worked and still work to run and maintain our canals.

Frederick R. Hobbs
Leighton Buzzard, March 2009

Chapter One

Early Days

I was born in Leighton Buzzard in 1933, into what was then a well-known local farming family. Inevitably, five years later, schooldays began, and I saw the Second World War from the perspective of a growing boy. Under the Labour Government, the leaving age from school was raised to fifteen in early 1947, just in time to catch me – and as my leaving date approached, I was of course expected to find work.

Although I had often played around both my father's and my uncle's farms, that kind of work did not really appeal to me. I did eventually obtain work with a local bakery – which I have to admit I quickly grew to hate! It wasn't so much the actual work as the heat, which regularly caused me severe headaches. And so my thoughts turned to the idea of working out of doors... But the story of the next few years had really begun some time earlier:

Whilst we were still at school, some friends and I had seen the film 'Painted Boats'. Until then, I knew very little about the canal, although it ran through the adjacent town of Linslade – I should explain that Linslade and Leighton Buzzard adjoined even then, although technically Linslade was in Buckinghamshire, while Leighton was in Bedfordshire, a situation which still pertains today. Two of my closest friends, Ralph and Bob and I, discussed the film and decided to take a bit of a closer look at this canal business.

Until then, my excursions into Linslade had consisted of the occasional walk to the railway station with my parents to take the train either for a visit to my sister who lived in Cogenhoe, near Northampton, or to an aunt and uncle who lived in Watford. And during the war, when we had double summer time, I would walk with my folks some Sunday evenings across the farmland and out onto the towpath, which we would follow to Linslade bridge, from whence it was a short walk back home.

So we three young fellows took to wandering along the canal, and at Leighton Lock we quickly got talking to the lock-keeper, a Mr Bambrook. Over the next little while, he showed us how the lock was worked, and initiated us into the use of a windlass to raise and lower the paddles. We learnt very much more from this kind and helpful gentleman – terms like pound and flight, staircase and summit – and he described to us the route of this canal, in former days known as the Grand Junction, with its two summit levels and two long tunnels.

From Brentford in Middlesex, where it opens into the River Thames, the boats would climb at every lock up as far as Cowroast, just north of Berkhamstead, where they would pass over the three-mile Tring Summit. Then, from the village of Bulbourne, they would descend again through Marsworth Locks, a flight of seven, and then continue down until they reached Fenny Stratford. A thirteen-mile pound took them on to Cosgrove, where the second climb began, through the flights of locks at Stoke Bruerne and Long Buckby to the second summit level at Braunston – a final descending flight of six then brought them to the northern end of the Grand Junction where it met the Oxford Canal. The Grand junction became part of the Grand Union system after 1929, when a number of the old private companies which had built the individual canals amalgamated for financial reasons, rather like what happened on the railways a few years earlier.

Now that we knew a bit about canal work, we itched for the experience of actually getting on board a narrowboat – and at last we got our chance. One Sunday evening, the three of us were walking along the towpath towards Leighton Lock when we saw a motor boat waiting above the lock. The lettering on the cabinside and the red, white and blue livery told us it was owned by the Grand Union Canal Carrying Company – nationalisation, when the boats would all be painted in the blue and yellow of the Transport Commission, was still some way off. A young girl was sitting in one side of the cabin doors reading a newspaper, and Ralph, being the boldest of us, called out:

'What're you waiting for, darling?' She looked up and replied:

'Me Mam 'n Dad're at the lock wi' two butties.' For anyone who doesn't know, a butty is an unpowered boat which was towed by the motor. Usually, one is paired up with each motor boat and the two work through wide locks, like those on the Grand Junction, together – the tradition of working boats in pairs actually goes back to the days when horses provided the motive power. But moving a spare boat was itself not so unusual – on this occasion, the extra butty was on its way to the G.U.C.C.Co. depot at Bulls Bridge to be docked.

All three of us ran towards the lock to see if we could help. The boatman was there with his wife and older daughter. We gave them what help we could, and then to our surprise he invited us aboard, introducing himself as Alf Best – I was later to discover that he was commonly known to his fellow-boatmen as 'Bessie'!

As time progressed, we three continued our excursions to the canal. Before long Ralph, who was the oldest by a couple of years, left school, and, after one or two unsuccessful jobs gained work with local wharf owner who also ran some narrowboats. L.B. (Laurence Bernard) Faulkner had begun his business at Charity Wharf in Linslade around 1910, with horse-drawn boats, although by this time he was running pairs of motors and butties. Faulkners had for many years brought coal to Leighton, unloading at what is still known as Brantom's Wharf. Thomas Brantom was a coal, corn and forage merchant who also had a shop in Leighton Buzzard High Street – the wharf no longer exists, although the name survives.

Another cargo carried by Faulkners, and other carriers in the area, was sand. For almost a century, the sand industry around

Leighton Buzzard had been controlled by two companies – these were George Garside, and Joseph Arnold and Sons. Both had at one time their own fleets of boats; the last pair of Garside's ceased work in 1950. On the south side of Linslade, Garsides had a quarry from which sand was brought to the boats by a narrow-gauge railway – this spot was known as the Boat-Hole, although there was no actual inlet or basin. Another carrier who took sand from the Boat-Hole was Alan Harvey-Taylor, based in Aylesbury.

North of the present-day town of Linslade and near to the village of Old Linslade, stands canal bridge number 110. Adjacent to this bridge can be seen the remains of a dock, where sand was loaded for the Birmingham area out of two-wheeled carts – and here I have a family connection! My grandfather was not only a farmer but also a carter, and had something approaching a monopoly of carting in the Leighton area, and among his jobs was the carrying of sand from the quarry in the nearby village of Heath to this dock, known as the Sand-Hole. To many, the bridge is still known as Sand-Hole Bridge.

During this period, while I was still at school, Ralph and I would spend our Saturdays and summer evenings along the towpath, trying to get ourselves a ride. If we were lucky, we might be taken as far as Wolverton, where we could climb some steps and cross the road to the railway station to get home. Or maybe to Berkhamstead, in the other direction.

Sometimes I would go alone; and thus it was that I met George Smith and his then wife Sonia. Known as 'Sonny' by the boaters, she had come to the boats during the war as one of the volunteers, the so-called 'Idle Women', and stayed on when she married George. I rode with them a number of times – George always let me steer his boat, the 'Cairo', up to the Tring Summit where I could get off by one of the bridges close to Tring station, and he would always give me ten shillings, quite a sum for a young lad in those days, for my help.

Among the others I met around this time were Jim and Doris Collins – both Jim and George worked for the Samuel Barlow Coal Company. And so both Ralph and I, in our different ways, began to learn how to work the boats and how to operate their various engines.

It was during this time that I first became familiar with what is still my all-time favourite engine, the Bolinder. My love affair began one bitter winter's day when Ralph, Bob and I had walked across the farmland to the canal. Reaching the towpath, we saw a pair of empty Ovaltine boats heading for Grove Lock, the last as you approach Leighton Buzzard from the south. We caught the eye of the boatman, who invited us aboard; he took one look at our frozen faces and said:

'Go in the injun-'ole, it's warm in theer!' Inside was this huge single-cylinder engine, thumping away at a steady pace with its characteristic hollow-sounding 'tonk-tonk-tonk' exhaust note, resplendent with dark green paint and gleaming brass. These engines were built in Sweden, and were the first to be used successfully in canal boats, from around 1910. Strictly speaking, they were semi-diesels, running on heavy oil (gas-oil to the boaters), and the starting procedure, as we learnt later, was something to behold.

To start, the Bolinder had to be pre-heated using a built-in blow-lamp – the air bottle was attached to the crankcase, and the nozzle mounted on the cylinder-head where it was directed onto a metal plug which led to the hot-bulb, protruding into the cylinder. It took about half an hour to suitably heat up the bulb – whilst this was going on, there being no oil sump on the engine, a small tank had to be filled with lubricating oil which then drips onto the various moving parts when the engine is running. Once properly hot, the engine was primed via the injector pump, the flywheel turned to the right position and a spring-loaded pin pushed out. Throwing your weight onto this pin spun the engine past compression, and with any luck it would fire and begin to run on its own, a procedure known to the boatmen as 'kicking-off'.

With a few later exceptions, the Bolinders used on the canal had no gearbox. With no other form of brakes, the only way to stop a boat is to reverse the propeller; with the Bolinder, that meant reversing the entire engine! Being a single-cylinder, two-stroke, that's not such an impossibility as might be thought. On a boat, the Bolinder had four controls: from left to right, the Reversing Rod, the Speed Wheel, the Clutch Rod and the Oil Rod – the Speed Wheel and the Oil Rod between them controlled the engine speed. To go astern, you had to slow the engine right down and disengage the clutch. Then, pulling back the Reversing Rod brought in a second injection pump which gave the engine a shot of fuel before the piston reached top dead centre – this would make it fire early, forcing the piston back down hard and reversing the direction of the flywheel. Re-engaging the clutch would then set the propeller turning backwards. You had to push the Reversing Rod back in smartly, though, or it would cause the engine to stop altogether, in which case the boat would career on, effectively out of control, with detrimental effects upon itself and anything which happened to be in the way.

Another company known for using Bolinders was Fellows, Morton and Clayton Ltd. Formed towards the end of the nineteenth century, they began with horse-drawn boats and steamers, but later switched to motor boats. One of the canal's biggest carrying companies, they were running over a hundred motor boats, all fitted with Bolinders, when they sold out to British Transport Waterways in 1949.

Climbing back out of the engine-hole, warmed and revived, we thanked the boatman, who gave his name as Charlie Carter. He and his brother Joe ran two out of the three remaining pairs of Ovaltine boats – the third was worked by Arthur Stokes and his family, but Arthur's motor, the 'Mimas', had a two-cylinder National engine of the type favoured by the old Grand Union company.

In the course of our canal explorations, we all soon became familiar with the many other types of engines which were commonly used in the boats – Petters, Nationals, Gardners and Listers. George Smith's motor had a Lister; two of the Barlow's boats we came to know were fitted with twin cylinder Gardners. One was the 'Gort', worked by the Beechey brothers, George and Albert until they both married, when George moved to work for S.E.Barlow. I should explain: There were two Barlow companies, quite separate but run by members of the same family. The Samuel Barlow Coal Company was based at Braunston, and known as the 'Limited', while S.E.Barlow ran out of Tamworth in Staffordshire, and were commonly known as 'Essie'.

George Beechey moved to S.E.Barlow to join his in-laws, whom I had also got to know – they were the Granthams, Mrs May Grantham, her daughter Liz and sons Joe and Ernie. Also among my new friends were two brothers, both working for the 'Limited'; they were Albert and Ernie Wilson, and I rode many times with both of them. Albert had the 'Neptune', fitted with a 25-horsepower Bolinder, one of the later ones with a gearbox, while Ernie's 'Prince' had the older 15-horespower type with no gearbox. I shall be eternally grateful to Ernie, for it was he who taught me how to work the Bolinder engine. Ralph, working for L.B.Faulkner's, had also learnt to drive a Bolinder, and this joint ability stood us in good stead on one of our Saturday excursions!

We were on the towpath that day, when two single motor boats came along. They were the 'Kestrel' and the 'Lion', both belonging to Fellows, Morton and Clayton. We were duly invited aboard for a ride, and intended to go with them only as far as Fenny Stratford – the boatmen were George Aldred on the Kestrel and Bill Hough on the Lion. We helped to work them as far as Fenny, when Bill told us that neither of them had had the time to eat since early morning. Would we like to go a bit farther, steering the boats while they had something in one of the cabins? Would we! We jumped at the chance, and took the boats almost all the way along the thirteen-mile pound, finally leaving them at Wolverton.

When they changed the school leaving age in 1947, Bob was one of the lucky ones who was not affected, and he soon dropped out of our canal trips once he was working. And with Ralph also at work, more and more I found myself out on my own, except for the odd summer evening. On these solitary excursions I met many other boat people – Bill Whitlock and his family, and another family by the name of Rice, who both worked for the 'Limited'; Jack Powell, and Joe Bray junior who at that time worked with another young chap. Then there was the Nixon family – the two boys, Jim and Ben, worked together – and Alec Purcell, Sid McDonald and Alf Wright, who all worked for Faulkners.

I began to get quite friendly with some of the younger generation of boaters, among them John Wilson who worked for British Waterways with his parents, and Charlie Littlemore whose folks worked for 'Essie'. Alec Purcell's lad Ronnie; and a fellow who became one of my best mates was Freddie Bodley, whose parents were with Fellows, Morton and Clayton, soon to be with B.W., albeit on their old boats.

Another young boater I came to know was Wilf Townsend. He worked the 'Bootes' and the 'Ironside' with his Uncle Alf – They with Wilf's late father had owned the two boats and mostly worked them on the Oxford Canal and down the Thames as far as Reading. Coming from that part of the world, they all had strong West Country accents, whereas mostly the boaters spoke with an odd mixture of London and West Midland, with a smattering of Oxford thrown in.

One of Wilf's favourite expressions, when he saw another pair coming towards us, was:

'Look owt, 'ere comes a baarrge!' He delighted in taking the mickey – most people 'on the bank' then referred to the boats as 'barges'. Sadly, many still do, although the correct term is 'narrowboat' – a barge is a wide craft, more often used on rivers or around the docks. I'd then get my own back by pretending surprise and saying:

'I've never seen a barge!'

Chapter Two

The Humphries

Now it was late 1948. For some years I had been enjoying these experiences, travelling around the canals of my locality; but things were about to change!

Ralph and I had planned one of our evening trips out but he failed to turn up at my house. I was rather peeved, and went around to his home, only to have his father tell me he was out. Later that evening he called, to tell me he had got a job with a family by the name of Skinner, working on a pair of Barlows boats. Was I envious!

I knew the Skinners, having met them some time before. The boatman's name was Jack, and with him he had his wife Rose and their little daughter, Joyce. Jack's motor was the 'Kent', fitted with a 15-horsepower Bolinder; his butty was the 'Forget-Me-Not'. Rose was the second daughter of a Mr Hone, from Banbury, who had in the past been a Number One, the colloquial term for an owner-boatman, and the 'Forget-Me-Not' had been one of his boats. Jack was the nephew of another well-known number one, Joe Skinner, who still worked his own horse-drawn boat, the 'Friendship', with his wife (another Rose), on the Coventry and Oxford Canals. Their boat still survives, and can be seen today preserved on dry land in the Boat Museum at Ellesmere Port in Cheshire.

Jack's parents also worked for Barlows, and all of them had appeared as extras in that film which had started my love of the canals, 'Painted Boats'. Jack and his wife had done the legging scene through Blisworth Tunnel, and his dad, also Jack, had played the lock-keeper at Stoke Bruerne.

In the course of our conversation that night, Ralph said:

'Well, you ain't working – why not try it?' That set me thinking, and I soon came to the same conclusion – why not?

A lovely sunny morning not long after found me at Church Lock, the second south of Leighton. The lock had gained its name from the tiny church close by, which is all that remains of a one-time Saxon village. Most of the locks along this stretch were known by names which originated with the boaters – the next one uphill (going south, in other words) was by the village of Slapton, and known as Neal's Lock after a previous lock-keeper; indeed, there was still a Mr Neal there in those days. A little further south, a close pair were known as Corkett's Two for a similar reason; the three locks north of Leighton and nowadays referred to as Soulbury were always ''Ammond Three', after the nearby village of Stoke Hammond, and the next single lock down (going north) to us was always Talbot's Lock.

I'd been there about an hour when the peace was disturbed by the heavy beat of a boat engine. The dull thud marked it in my mind as a single-cylinder Petter; the boats, when they came into view, were empty and running breasted up along the two-mile, as that pound was known, from Slapton.

They ran into the lock, and as I waited to close the inside (towpath side) top gate, the woman on the butty, a rather good-looking blonde, smiled and called out:

'Are you goin' to do that for me?' I noticed a young boy and girl aboard as well; the boatman, a short stocky chap, closed his gate and called across to me:

'Wi' boats?' He naturally assumed that I was lock-wheeling, but when I answered him No, he asked where I lived. When I told him, he said:

''Op on then 'n we'll give you a roide!'

Once we'd passed the next lock at Grove, he introduced himself as 'Bill 'Oomphries' (Humphries). His wife was Oiris (Iris), and the children Moike and Jean; their boats were the 'Franklyn' and the 'Lily of the Valley', owned by S.E.Barlow. They were on their way to the dock at Bedworth, on the Coventry Canal, to have a new set of blades (a new propeller) fitted, so they were in no great hurry. It was while we were travelling along the Leighton pound that he unwittingly gave me the title for this book:

'They call oos droy land sailors, 'ave you 'eerd on oos?' Then suddenly he asked: 'Would you loike to come wi' oos for the wikend?' You can imagine my reply! But:

'I'll have to let my parents know.'

'Roit. We'm stoppin' a whoile, so you go 'n see yer Mam 'n Dad, 'n we'll wait for you.'

My home was about two miles from the canal, but I made it there and back within the hour.

And so we set off. Below Leighton lock, I sat on the butty with Iris, chatting and having a bite to eat and a cup of what Ralph always called 'Boatman's Tea', strong and sweet, and topped off with condensed milk. Iris knew Ralph, and she asked me about myself, and why I liked the boats so much. She told me that she too had come 'off the bank', having lived in Oxford and met up with Bill after some kind of personal trouble. Bill was then working a single horse-boat on the Oxford Canal, and after being given a motor they had continued up to then working along the Oxford and the Coventry, which explained why I had not come across them before.

As we passed over the aqueduct near Wolverton, Iris remarked:

'I wouldn't want to fall down there, would you?' Not likely!

On through Cosgrove Lock and along the Stoke pound which took us past the village of Yardley Gobion, and soon we were approaching the flight of seven Stoke Bruerne locks where we could breast up once more. Bill kept the boats abreast out of the top lock as he intended staying there for the night. We tied up just past the Boat Inn, which had also featured in 'Painted Boats', and Bill asked:

'D'yer drink, chap? Only Oi'm thinkin' abart a pint.' I was still under age, but I did go with him for a pint! After a bit of supper with the family, I went across to the cabin of the 'Franklin' for what was to become the first of many nights spent sleeping aboard.

Like the Bolinder, the old single Petter had to be pre-heated with a blow-lamp. Then, after being primed and having the lubricators checked, the flywheel was swung over in the same way until after one final swing the engine would fire. But with a gearbox fitted, the Petter had only two controls, the 'clutch' for forwards and reverse and a speed-wheel for the engine revs. That morning, once ready, we set off for the few hundred yards from the village to the southern end of the Blisworth Tunnel.

By this time, many narrowboats were fitted with electric lighting both for the headlamps and inside the cabins. The batteries were usually kept under the sidebeds, the one on the motor boat being charged by a dynamo on the engine, and the two swapped over from time to time so that the butty one didn't get too flat. But Bill's boats still relied on oil lamps, so after our breakfast he'd placed an oil-burning headlamp on each fore-deck. When running loaded, they would usually be placed on the top-plank with the handle hooked over the mast – the lamps themselves were generally quite ornate, painted with roses and often the boat's name.

I stayed on the butty, talking to Iris. When empty, the butty usually needs little steering as it is towed directly behind the motor on cross-straps, making the whole ensemble act rather like an articulated lorry. Only in some turns, where the 'ellum (rudder) could knock on broken coping stones and become dislodged – and getting it back into place was no easy task – or when meeting other boats when the draw on the water could suck the boats together, would it need an occasional corrective nudge. Anyway, on we chugged, the Franklyn's exhaust echoing off the dark cavernous walls.

Once back into the daylight, Iris asked if I would relieve Bill so that he could remove the headlamps. Now – that meant getting from boat to boat whilst on the move. No easy feat! Running empty, the butty sits light and high out of the water, while the motor, weighed down by the engine and drivetrain, sits on a slope, deep in at the stern. Walking along the butty's planks, I dropped down onto the fore-deck. From there I had to reach down and grasp the ram's head of the motor and gently lower myself down several feet onto the counter.

I took over from Bill, and he went forward to remove the motor's headlamp, then back past me to negotiate the hazard in the opposite direction to get aboard the butty. Once there, he left me in charge of the motor for quite a while – we were now on the long Blisworth pound, all sixteen miles of it.

In those days there were a number of places on the Junction which the boaters didn't much care for. One such was at Bourne End, below Berkhamstead, where there was a weir on the outside of a turn, which meant you had to go as close as you dared in order to negotiate the bend. Another was Simpson Bridge, below Fenny Lock, which was in the middle of an 'S' bend. You would always slow down when entering a bridge-hole, because the water often wasn't all that deep and the propeller could push all the water out of the bridge leaving the stern of the motor high and dry, and then all kinds of chaos could ensue! Running loaded, the butty was likely to come up and ram the motor, and unless you were very lucky that would result in the towrope getting caught in the blades. And that would mean groping under the stern with the cabin-shaft in order to free it again. The S-bend at Simpson just made this operation that much more delicate.

Another such place was at Stowe Hill, on the Blisworth pound – and that was where I got the Franklyn stemmed up! You have to remember that the boats were all flat-bottomed, so that if you ran onto a mud-bank no amount of going astern would stop you in time to prevent getting well and truly stuck – which is what the boaters meant by getting stemmed up. Stowe Hill Bridge is another one right on an S-bend, and, because the boats would always go around the outside of a bend, you'd find a mud-bank tended to build up on the inside, the silt getting blown over that way by the combination of rudder and propeller as the motor boat turned. Anyway, I cut the corner too fine, hit the mud and ended up with the Franklyn's fore-end up the high bank on the outside. Bill quickly came to my rescue with a shaft, and soon the boat was back where it should have been.

'Bloimy, Oi thought you were goin' 'ill-cloimbin'!' was his comment.

A while later we came to the locks at Long Buckby. The boaters always knew these as the 'Bugby' flight, although nowadays British Waterways like us to think of the lower ones as Whilton locks. Above the top lock is the Braunston summit, and the junction where the Leicester section turns off; in the top lock, Bill refitted the headlamps as we would soon have to pass through the Braunston Tunnel. Beyond the tunnel lay the northern-most locks of the Grand Junction, leading down again into the village.

Bill, seemingly once more out to prove that he was in no hurry, tied up near the boatyard which was one of the Limited's depots, and my weekend with them was over. But as I was getting ready to leave, he asked if I would like to come and work with them. Needless to say, I was delighted at the prospect, but I had to get home to let my parents know – I walked up to Braunston Station (this was well before Dr Beeching!) and caught a train to Northampton, and another from there to Leighton.

On the following morning, with a few personal possessions, I set off down to the canal in the hope of getting a lift on some boats which could take me to Bedworth, where I was to meet the Humphries. My mother wasn't too happy about the whole idea, and nor were my two elder brothers, but Dad, more or less resigned to what I proposed to do, just said:

'If that's what you want, go on then.'

I arrived at Leighton Lock about 8.30am. It was quite some time before any empty boats came along, and when they did I was surprised to see that they were a British Waterways pair – usually, BW's boats would have a back-load from Brentford or Limehouse for the northward trip. These were ex-FMC boats, the motor still running the Bolinder engine. I asked the boatman if he could take me to Bedworth, and told him why I was going there. He refused, and as I could see he had his wife and son and daughter with him, I took that as being the reason why.

I started to walk along the towpath, hoping someone I knew like Jim Collins or Ernie Wilson would come along, and as I neared the swing-bridge below the lock, the boats caught up with me. The boatman seemed to have had a change of heart – he called out:

'Come on, chap – 'ave yer a roide!' I wondered if Mr Bambrook had put in a word for me! Soon we were chatting like old friends, and needless to say I helped out where I could. At 'Ammond Three, Bill Garner, the lock-keeper, called out to me:

''Avin' another day out then?'

'No' I replied, 'I'm going to work with Bill Humphries!'

By this time I had joined the son on the motor boat, and he asked me:

'Know Bill orl roight then?' He meant Bill Garner:

'Yes' I told him, 'I've known him for several years now.' I went on to tell him of my expeditions on the canal over the years, until, as we were nearing Talbot's Lock, he said:

'Oi bet you can't tek us into the lock!'

They all seemed quite surprised when I happily put the Bolinder into reverse and slipped the butty loose.

At Fenny Stratford I was invited onto the butty for a meal, which almost by tradition was washed down with a cup of that great boatman's tea. As we travelled around the Fenny pound I found myself being congratulated on my prowess at steering and my handling of the Bolinder. Looking down from the aqueduct as we approached Cosgrove I was reminded of Iris' words of a few days before.

After leaving Cosgrove Lock I was back on the motor and allowed to do some more steering. Very soon, it seemed, we reached Stoke Bruerne where I helped with the locks, and then we were off through the tunnel – with electric lights this time! I stayed on the butty through the tunnel, only returning to the motor at Long Buckby, this time with the captain; along the Blisworth pound, we passed several pairs heading south with coal for some of the various mills, among them boatmen with whom I had ridden at one time or another – and we met Ralph and the Skinners.

Eventually we were up to the top of Buckby and onto the Braunston summit. I was steering, but then the boatman himself took over for the passage through the tunnel itself while I sat in the cabin. I suppose most people now know that due to a miscalculation when it was being built, Braunston Tunnel has a distinct kink near the southern end – the abrupt appearance of an intruding wall, looming up in the headlight, can give the unwary the horrifying feeling of running into a dead-end!

Below Braunston Locks and past the various boatyards you come to the junction with the Oxford Canal. We held straight on, heading up the North Oxford towards Coventry, but as we passed the junction the boatman pointed the other way and announced:

'That go to Axford – Dahn theer is where we tarns orf for Brummagem.' Back then, Brummagem was a colloquial term for the City of Birmingham used both by the boaters and those on the bank. One of the earliest sites of the Industrial Revolution, Birmingham is sometimes known as England's Engine House – the many coalmines in the region along with sources of iron ore helped to transform it from a little Warwickshire town into what it is today, once the canals came along.

As darkness began to fall, I noticed some lights in the distance. These were set on the tops of the wireless masts close to Hillmorton, a suburb of Rugby where the canal passed through. We tied for the night at the top of the locks there; as there was no spare room in either of the cabins, the captain gave me some blankets and suggested I could sleep under the motor's cratch. It was a warm night, and after such a long day I was soon fast asleep.

'Toime to get up, chap!' It was the boatman's son: 'Coom over to the butty 'n 'ave some snap!' After breakfast, he asked if I would like to watch him start up.

The locks at Hillmorton are very unusual – there are six in all, but arranged in three pairs, side by side, so you have two narrow locks for each rise and fall. Each pair is connected by a culvert with a paddle, so if things are co-ordinated right, a downhill motor boat can draw the paddle and part-fill the opposite lock to half-raise an uphill motor going the other way. With the centre paddle closed again, the two locks are finally filled or emptied using the normal paddles, letting the motors out and leaving each one set for the two opposing butties to use.

It was below Hillmorton Locks that I saw my first canal horse. It was a beautiful white creature, its harness gleaming, brightly painted wooden bobbins along its sides and brasses sparkling in the morning sun. The bobbins were there to prevent the towing harness chafing the horse's flanks; behind its rump was a wooden bar similar to those seen on horse-drawn ploughs. This was known as the spreader – one end of the towline was attached to this, and the other to the mast of the boat. In this instance, the family were running two boats – the second, still called a butty, was towed behind the first, but not with the usual type of towline. On the butty's planks, above each of the stands, was a wooden block with a central aperture. The towline was passed through a pulley at the top of the mast, then through these, and finally tied onto a T-stud screwed into the top of the cabin in front of the steerer. This method meant that control of the towline was left to the person on the butty – some boaters used the same idea for towing with a motor, when it could be even more useful because if you had to slow down suddenly, the butty steerer could haul in the towrope and so stop it getting wrapped around the blades. These boats, owned by S.E.Barlows, were run by the Taylors, brothers Joe and Walter and their two sisters; they were on their way to Oxford with coal. Another sister, it happened, was married to Ben Johnson who worked for the Limited, and I had previously ridden with him a number of times.

Later that day we met Joe and Rose Skinner, with the 'Friendship'. Joe's motive power took the form of his old mule, and as with all the boat horses that I saw, Dolly was done up in the same colourful and spectacular way. In long pounds, horseboatmen would often hang a metal bowl from the collar of the harness, filled with oats, so that the horse (or mule) could feed as it trudged along. This was the nose-tin, usually as brightly-painted as any other part of the boat's equipment. You wouldn't want to stop along the way for the horse to feed, because there would probably be other boats behind, maybe going to the same place, and if you let them past they would be unloaded first, making you late. For a number one like Joe, that would mean losing money, because he only got paid by the trip. Another consideration was that you needed to reach somewhere for the night where the horse could be stabled – its health and comfort were a prime concern! Most canalside inns had stables, as did the wharves and unloading places because many of them would have their own road horses for local deliveries. Brantom's Wharf, which I've mentioned before, was one such.

At last we came in sight of the power station at Longford, about a mile from Hawkesbury Junction where the Oxford and Coventry Canals meet. Known to the boaters as Coventry Light, a few boats were unloading there – a pair of Barlows, and a couple 'Joey' boats. Joeys were commonly used around the Birmingham area – day-boats, whose crews lived on the bank and returned home every night. Some had a small cabin, just used for a 'brew-up' during the day; usually they were double-ended, and the 'ellum could be moved from one end to the other to save the effort of turning the whole boat around. Incidentally – let me correct a common mispronunciation! 'Winding' a boat sounds like what you might do to a baby, not to a clock. Like a windy day.

Hawkesbury Junction itself, which we reached soon after, is commonly known to everyone on the cut, even today, as Sutton's Stop. I was told the following tale about how that nickname came to be: In the early days of the canals, some boats travelling long distances such as Liverpool or Manchester to London, were licensed to work non-stop. These were known as 'Fly-Boats'; they would change horses at various pre-determined points – many were operated by Pickfords, a company still well-known today, although they left the canals in the 1840s! Tolls had to be paid to travel the canals – the boats were gauged at stops along the way, their load being calculated by the depth they rode in the water, measured by the toll-clerk with a rod that checked the amount of dry side showing above water. Reference to a set of record books then allowed him to charge the appropriate fee for the weight and type of cargo. The most important toll offices were at the junctions between different canals – boats coming south would be gauged at Fazeley entering the Coventry Canal, and then again at Hawkesbury to turn onto the Oxford. And then at Braunston, and so on.

Some boatmen, in order to avoid paying the tolls, would try to sneak through the gauging points under cover of darkness. The story goes that the general manager of the Oxford Canal then was a Mr Sutton, and it was he who cottoned on to this ruse. It came to light because the boats which travelled regularly on a given route would become known to the toll clerks, and if a particular boat hadn't been seen for a while, he began to check up with the boat's owners. If it turned out that the boat should have gone through, it was pretty obvious what was going on! Mr Sutton then had a large wooden boom fitted across the canal at the stop place, on the Coventry side of the junction, which could be locked at night – and the toll clerks were told to do just that before they went home each evening.

Once we'd passed through 'Sutton's', we headed on towards Bedworth, where the boatman slowed down to allow me to jump from their butty onto Bill's.

'Good Luck!' he called, and with a clatter from their engine and a swish of the butty's 'ellum they were gone.

I was welcomed on board with something to eat, and then I took my things up to the Franklyn's cabin. I say 'up' advisedly – the boat was in the drydock, resting on trestles, and so to get aboard I had to descend a ladder into the dock and then climb another onto the boat – before I did so, I looked up and for the first time realised just how big these boats really were! The new blades had not yet been fitted, as there was some other work to be done on the propeller shaft, and a new stern bush needed to be fitted. This was the short metal tube through which the shaft protruded from the inside of the hull – if the stern bush became eroded from the constant spinning of the shaft, water would begin to seep in and accumulate under the floor of the cabin. The prop shaft ran under the cabin floor, its sections joined by couplings – this is why the cabin is taller on a motor boat than on a butty.

Some boats had bilge pumps, run off the engine, which would pump out any excess water, but Bill's boats did not. Instead, they had a hand pump which looked like a long, heavy pipe set in the back end of the hold. It would be primed by lifting it out and dipping it in the canal, and then, set up in place again, the handle was heaved up and down and the water pumped out through a spout which of course had to face out over the side – rather like a huge stirrup pump.

After depositing my goods and chattels in the Franklyn's cabin, I returned to the butty, and Iris and I went into Bedworth to do a bit of shopping. The rest of the day was spent on odd jobs – I got the task of mopping the butty down. Mopping off was a regular chore on the boats, especially after loading and unloading – all the boaters I knew were very proud of their boats and keen to keep them looking smart, and so the paintwork was always kept clean. All the boats carried a long-handled rag mop, usually kept on the cabin-top with the handle resting through the handles of the water-cans. The cans themselves were large, holding either two or three gallons, and pretty heavy when they were full, and almost always highly decorated. Kept in front of the chimney on the cabin-top, they were the boaters fresh-water supply – taps to fill them were mostly found by the locks, or at stops such as Sutton's.

On the subject of decoration, inside the cabins you would almost universally find a castle scene on the table-cupboard door, and two smaller ones at the top of the stern doors. The recessed centre panels of the doors usually sported a swag of roses, with more on the side panel just inside the right-hand door as you look in from the counter. Butties and horse-boats generally had a back-end door which opened from the bed-hole into the hold, and these were often painted in similar fashion; I have even seen the same done on the connecting door inside some motors. The outside of a boat was of course painted in the owner's livery, but even then most butties had a small square panel at the stern-end of the cabin which would often bear a castle scene. Decoration like this was much less in evidence on the bigger fleets' boats, such as the Grand Union Carrying Company.

Very soon it was time for bed – steadily I climbed up to my cabin and before long was lost in dreamland. Next morning, I awoke to the sound of Bill calling me to come over to the butty for breakfast.

By this time the workmen had arrived, and by mid-morning the Franklyn was ready; the dock was filled from the canal through two large paddles and the boat at last floated out.

We had orders to load at Griff Colliery, so Bill got the engine started while I put on the two short cross-straps. Griff was a typical mining village of the time, coal-dust and slag-heaps everywhere. It stood near the Nuneaton-Coventry road, and had its own canal basin which was reached via a short tree-lined arm whose entrance was under a bridge with a very low arch. So low, that boats could not get under if the cratch was in place. Taking it down entailed removing the forward top-cloth and top-plank, the false cratch which was like a large letter 'A' sitting between the gunwales and the plank, and then the triangular deck-board itself – solid timber, and no lightweight thing, believe me! However, at last we came out into a wide expanse of water where several pairs were loading, the coal being brought to the wharf in sixteen-ton railway wagons. To load, a steel chute was propped up into the wagon with its other end over the boat's gunwale, and the coal shovelled down – some of the loaders were ex-boatmen. Loading already that day were a couple of pairs of Barlows (Limited), another S.E. pair, and two or three joeys, also belonging to 'Essies'.

As there was no chance of loading before lunch, we had our meal before changing into old clothes and getting the boats ready. Soon our turn came, and gradually the Franklyn began to sink lower in the water as the coal was shovelled in. The motor had no side cloths, so once it was full all Bill and I had to do was replace the cratch, planks and uprights. He reckoned it had once had a covered hold, like the Clayton's 'tar boats' which then still collected gas tar from the old coal-burning gas works – they had a flat wooden deck over the hold, with hatches through which the liquid load was pumped in and out. The Lily of the Valley, in contrast, did have side cloths, and these we raised once she was loaded. Top cloths were rarely used when carrying coal, unless it was specified as 'dry coal'.

Once we were ready, we headed back down the arm, out onto the Coventry Canal and turned south towards Hawkesbury. At the junction, the Coventry goes straight on into the city itself, but to turn onto the northern Oxford and head towards London means negotiating a 180-degree turn under a cast-iron side bridge. This is a very sharp turn, partly because of the stop-place I mentioned earlier; and coming under the bridge you would often encounter a motor being refuelled outside the pub which stood by the basin on the Oxford side of the junction. Harry Nelson, publican of the Greyhound, also supplied diesel and engine-oil, while his wife worked in the little shop.

The usual practice was to slow the motor down and then loose off the butty. The motor would be wound up to start going around the turn, and then shut down again as the stern came under the bridge to avoid dragging in the shallow water there. Once through, the speed was increased again to bring the boat around towards the lock, where it would be gauged. With that done, the motor would be run out of the lock and then backed up against the top gate, the steerer tying the boat by its stern to the handrail while he went back to help with bowhauling the butty around the turn with a line from the mast. The butty could then be gauged in its turn.

Once all this was done we moved on again – but not far, only about a mile to Tusses Bridge near Longford to tie for the night.

Chapter Three

The Journeys

The next day we set off along the 'Morton pound – and that is where my boating days could have come to an untimely end! Bill asked me to mop-off the motor, a job which is normally done starting at the fore-end and working back along the boat. The mop would be dipped in the canal and every surface to be mopped given a good soaking; then the mop would be wrung out by rolling it rapidly between the hands or arms, a process known as wringling, and then used to dry off the worst of the water.

Anyway, I didn't feel brave enough to walk along the planks. On an empty boat, if you slipped and fell you would end up in the bottom of the hold, at the worst with a few cuts and bruises – but on a loaded boat, you'd land on the load with a good chance of rolling or bouncing over the side and ending up in the water. I managed it anyway! Walking on the coal, I must have stepped on a rounded lump; and the next moment I found myself swimming alongside. From down here, the Franklyn looked even bigger than it had in the dry-dock – now I knew how the crew of a tug-boat must feel when they are towing a really big ship! Bill immediately put the engine into neutral and reached down with his strong hands to pull me back on board.

After drying myself off and a change of clothes I retired to the butty for a while. There, Iris told me if I put my wet clothes aside she would get them washed for me as soon as she could. There were places around the canals where you could leave things to be laundered, but most of the boatwomen preferred to do their own washing, and they would take the opportunity whenever they were tied up for any length of time. A fire would be set up on the bank and the wash-tub filled with water and placed over it, and then the clothes put in to boil. In those days there weren't so many washing powders as we have today (I can only remember Persil or Oxydol) and most women, even housewives on the bank, used Sunlight soap and plenty of scrubbing. Once clean, the clothes would be hung up on a long line from the butty's back-end to the mast, where the constant breeze would soon have them dry. Apart from my working clothes I had a smarter 'uniform' of a white shirt and black trousers which I would wear to go to the pub or for an outing, to the cinema for example. I still like to wear such a combination today.

That day we went as far as Fenny Stratford, tying up above the shallow lock. Very handy for the Red Lion, both pub and shop! Quite a few canal-side pubs then had a small shop – another popular one was at the 'Ammond three locks, then known as the Castle Inn. A quiet little place – not like today.

The following day we resumed our journey. A little way along the Water Eaton pound I stepped off to walk up and set Talbot's Lock; and there I was met by Ralph:

''Eer!' He said: ''Eer's somethin' to give yer a laugh! Last night we were headin' for Leighton, comin' down the Nag's Head, an' I was lock-wheelin'.' The Nag's Head Three are spaced-out locks, known as Seabrook nowadays by BW, near Ivinghoe, named by the boaters after a pub which vanished many years ago.

'Anyway' he continued 'I'd just got away from the middle lock when me bike jumped in the air. I shouted out "Christ!", a woman screamed, an' a bloke's voice yelled "Why don't you look where you're bloody goin'?" It were dark, an' I din't see them – they must 'ave been across the towpath! I got away bloody quick, din't 'ang about to see what they were doin!'

We plodded on through Leighton, to be gauged at Marsworth top lock with fifty-two tons – that had emptied a few wagons back at Griff! Downhill again through Berkhamstead to that dratted swing-bridge at Winkwell which carries the road across the canal. One member of the crew had to get off to wind the blessed thing open, and then close it as soon as the boats had passed through; but if you were short handed a quick toot on the horn would bring the landlord of the Three Horseshoes to the rescue. After Winkwell came one of the old hopping-off places from my riding days, at Boxmoor Lock. Below the lock lay a limejuice depot belonging to a Dutch firm; their boast was that their product went all the way by water, first on the Dutch canals, across the North Sea by ship, up the Thames by lighter and then along the Grand Union Canal by narrowboat.

Also below Boxmoor lay the five locks known as the 'New 'Uns'. When the Grand Junction was first built, it followed a different route just below Boxmoor, with four locks. But John Dickinson, who owned the paper-mills in that area complained about the navigation causing water shortages at the mills, and the canal company were forced to re-route that stretch. The new line necessitated a total of five locks – one at Two Waters, one at Apsley Mill, one at Frogmore, and two at Nash Mill, one above and one below. In my day a board joined the new and old towpaths just below the last new lock. Kings Langley Lock, which used to be number 69, was renumbered as 69A to accommodate the extra one, becoming in fact the seventieth lock from Braunston!

Below this lock stands the famous Ovaltine factory. For many years, Ovaltines had run their own fleet of boats, bringing coal to the factory from the Warwickshire coalfields – I mentioned going on Charlie Carter's pair earlier in my story – which were always immaculately turned out. I don't know if the famous beverage itself was ever despatched by canal! Barlows (the Limited) also brought coal to Kings Langley in my day.

By the time we'd reached this point the light was fading. Next came Home Park Lock, another named Five-Paddle, close by the West Coast Main Line of the railway from Euston, and then two close together known as Hunton Bridge Two, also easily seen from the trains – this is just by where the Watford Road meets the bypass. Now we were entering 'The Parks', the section of canal that passes through the estates of Lord Capel and the Earl of Essex – the next lock below Hunton Bridge is still called 'Lady Capel's' because, in the early days, the Earl's sister lived nearby.

It was dark now, and although I could hear the hum of traffic from the bypass, it felt quite eerie, and as we went on towards Cassio Bridge trees hung over the towpath like great shadows. When I was a child during World War Two I'd had an unsettling experience in the dark: I was about six, and had been to tea with a friend from school. Walking home after dark, with no street lamps or traffic lights, and the rare car or bus with their headlamps hooded in the blackout, even my home town seemed quite alien. To this day, I don't like darkened streets.

Cassio Bridge was our last lock for the day. I had been lock-wheeling, and now I was glad to get back on the boats. Soon we arrived at Croxley Mill, guided in by the light from a butty cabin as a boater looked out to see who it was that had turned up. We tied up, singled out against the towpath, because at this time barges (yes, real barges!) still worked up this far with rags or wood-pulp, or sometimes wood for a local timber-yard. Twelve feet wide, they were mostly horse-drawn, and the horses were just as finely dressed as any I had seen. At one time barges with families on board had worked up as far as Berkhamstead, but these ones were only run as day boats, like the joeys.

In the morning Bill and I put on our old clothes and set about stripping the boats ready for unloading. Ahead of us were three pairs – Jim Peasland with his Harvey-Taylor boats (I was quite pally with his son Maurice), Ron Wilson with a pair of S.E.Barlows, and Bill's brother Tom with B.W. (formerly Grand Union). While we were waiting another pair arrived – these were Limited boats, captained by Charlie Roberts, another acquaintance of mine.

When our turn came, we moved the boats along into position by shafting them. The boat's shafts were a kind of universal tool with a point and hook on one end; they could be used to propel the boats for short distances without the need to start the engine, or as I've mentioned before to push off from mud-banks. The hook often came in handy for dragging rubbish out of the blades, although if you were lucky this could be achieved by a quick shift into stern gear, known as chucking back.

Once in the unloading place, a large steel cable was attached to the shackle on the boat's side, and a belt-like conveyor fitted with metal buckets was lowered into the hold. As the coal was lifted out, the operator could draw the boat forward as needed by simply pushing switches. When the Franklyn was empty, we moved it out to allow the butty in. The cratch was stacked against the forward bulkhead, the uprights stored tidily beside it and the planks placed between the cross-beams. With the stands left in place, the boat's bottom could then be thoroughly swept out.

At last the butty was empty too. Bill climbed into the engine-hole whilst I shafted the boat alongside and breasted the pair up; with a thumping the Petter throbbed into life, and we went straight into the lock, fortunately left full by a loaded B.W. pair coming up. Once through, I stayed on the lockside while Bill winded the boats in the wide-hole below and brought them back in. With the lock full again, I got back on board and we started heading north. Up the next few pounds I had to go lock-wheeling, and I found the towpath under its overhanging trees a lot less unfriendly than it had seemed the previous night! Up towards Langley we began to meet other boats coming down, so I was able to go back on the boats and get on with other things, like mopping them off and polishing the chimney-rings.

That night we tied up above Marsworth, close to the entrance of the old Wendover arm. On our way down the flight the next morning, we met several pairs coming up – among them was Henry Hancock with his Garside boats, and then three Limited pairs, with Jim Collins, Ernie Wilson and Bill Whitlock in charge. And then later, on the Jackdaw pound below Leighton we passed the folks who had given me that lift to Bedworth. Pressing on we reached Stoke Bruerne – the boaters mostly referred to the village just as 'Stoke', rarely using the full name. Confusing, maybe, for some – easy to think they might have meant Stoke-on-Trent! Another confusing place-name was 'Thrupp': There's a village on the Oxford Canal by that name, but it was also a common diminutive for places ending in 'thorpe', like Castlethorpe on the Grand Junction. There were a couple of pairs already tied above the top lock, and Bill reckoned it would be the best idea to stop there with them.

Next morning, headlamps on, and we set off towards the tunnel and the long Blisworth pound. By now Bill had decided that I was capable of handling the Franklyn around the turns at Weedon, and even, later on, across the Braunston Summit and through the Braunston tunnel. That day we reached Sutton's where orders were waiting for us to load again at Griff, for Croxley once more.

It was on that run that trouble struck. We'd stopped below the paired locks of Hillmorton, and then the Franklyn's engine was reluctant to re-start. Bill gave it full throttle, much more than was usually needed, and even then it took several swings on the flywheel before it eventually fired. We struggled on, the aged Petter chugging and blowing smoke like an old and tired steamer, until above the top lock it gave up altogether.

'Booger!' said Bill: 'Oi'll go down to the yard an' arx 'em ter phone Barlows.'

Just after he got back, we heard the distinctive sound of an approaching Bolinder, and up the flight behind us came the Skinners and my old mate Ralph. They tied just in front of us, and Jack disappeared into our engine-hole.

'Peston rings. It must be peston trouble' he announced, emerging again – good with engines, was Jack. Eventually the fitters arrived from Glascote, and in short order the hot bulb and cylinder head were off. They turned the flywheel to bring the piston to the top of its travel, and Jack was proved to be right – worn piston rings! Fortunately, they had anticipated the problem and brought a spare piston with them. Part of the crankcase had to be removed in order to change it, but at last everything was put back together and the blow-lamp put on. The engine fired up, and I'd never heard it sound better.

Jack thought it would be a good idea if we buttied up, travelling together to help each other along, and we set off again, the Kent's Bolinder and the Franklyn's Petter rattling in harmony. We stayed together as far as Croxley where we were to unload – Jack was bound for Kearley and Tonge's factory, the famous 'Jam 'Ole' in Southall. We didn't see them again for a while, as he then had orders to load timber in Brentford to go to Leicester. But the trip together had given Ralph and I time to catch up, especially as we had all stopped in Leighton, allowing us both to pop home for a visit.

The next journey gave us a bit of a change: This time, we loaded at Baddesley Colliery, for Home Park Mill, another of the John Dickinson group. Baddesley was about half-way down the flight of narrow locks at Atherstone, on the Coventry Canal; on the way there we passed the entrances to both Griff and Newdigate, which lay up a short arm near Bedworth. Also along that stretch was the junction with the Ashby Canal, better known to the boaters as the Moira (or Mardy) cut – this twenty-mile lock free length went up to Measham, where the pottery came from, and where most of the coal for the Coventry Light was loaded.

The level pound from Sutton's to Atherstone (or 'Ariston') was a long one, and took us through the town of Nuneaton. Eventually we reached the top lock – being narrow, we had to run the motor down first and then bow-haul the butty after it. Baddesley turned out some of the finest coal in the West Midlands, and was the preferred supplier for Ovaltines. Sometimes boats had to wait outside the small basin until a pair came out to make room for them, but we were lucky as only one other pair was there, almost loaded. It looked as though we would have a good chance of loading before the men finished for the day.

As at Griff, the coal was shovelled in out of railway wagons. And we were indeed loaded in good time – we moved out again, taking the Franklyn up first and then bow-hauling the Lily of the Valley to the top of the locks, where we decided to stay for the night. We treated ourselves to a trip to the pictures, and saw a film called The Black Tent. Most of the next day I spent at one or the other of the tillers, on the motor around to Hawkesbury and then on the butty up to Hillmorton. No troubles this time, and within two days we were at Home Park, near Kings Langley.

A small inlet took us in to the mill itself. The elevator was brought out, and our work began – we had to shovel the coal over the gunwales, some four feet above the boat's floor, easy enough from the top of the load, but as we got closer to the bottom the harder it got! We were using the large number ten shovels; Iris joined in, as most of the boatwomen did – a boatman once said proudly to me:

'You ought ter see the wenches wi' a shovel an' a barrer!' That's a good old name for a working girl, going back to Tudor times but still in common use on the canals of the fifties!

It took us about two hours to shift the load, for which we were rewarded with three pounds per boat – not a lot for shovelling fifty-two tons of coal by hand. Small coal was usually known as 'peas', larger stuff as 'beans' and only really large blocks as 'coal' – and believe me, this was 'coal'! When the job was done and the boats tidied up we began our return journey, stopping overnight at Marsworth and then going on to Fenny, where Jack was tied up, heading down loaded. Ralph and I had once spent evenings together in Bletchley, so now we decided to go and visit some of our old haunts, including a cafe which we used to frequent.

When we got back to Hawkesbury we received orders for a short run, from Griff to the 'Light' at Longford. Not too bad, but a bit dull after our long trips. On the same run was Ted Barrett and his family – they had worked for the Limited but were now with S.E.Barlow. They had two older lads, Ted junior and Ken, with whom I became quite friendly.

After a few more runs to the Light we resumed our trips up the Junction. Our first trip was to Home Park – our orders seemed to alternate between there and Croxley – and this was not to go without incident! Somewhere along the way, the Franklyn started to shudder, and a rattle emanated from under the cabin floor.

'Coupling' Bill announced, pulling in to the side: 'Go an' put the injun out, whoile Oi tek the floor up.' The boaters always spoke of 'putting the engine out' rather than 'stopping'; I climbed down into the engine-hole and stopped the Petter with the foot-lever which also served to prime the engine before starting.

With the coupling sorted out, we only got as far as Old Linslade when the next mishap occurred. A little way north of the Globe Inn there is a sharp inside turn. Bill was steering when 'wallop!'

the ’ellum hit a submerged coping stone. The ram’s head was weaving about like a drunk heading home from the pub because the rudder had jumped out of its socket. Once more we pulled into the bank. Guess who got wet? Whilst I did my utmost to guide the blessed thing back into place Bill jiggled the ram’s head around. This was done again with the engine put out – if Bill had inadvertently knocked the clutch in, yours truly could have ended up as mincemeat!

After almost a year with Bill and Iris, I was getting restless. Not that I was fed up, nor that I had fallen out with them, but coming from the bank I wanted to see more of canal life, and when Bill told me he was going to work around the Light again, my decision was made. After one more trip with them, I left them where we had first met, at Church lock. I was eventually to work with them again, but not for many years to come.

Chapter Four

"Skipper"

Having left the Humphries, I soon obtained work in Leighton Buzzard with a small engineering works. Sad to say, it didn't work out – it was no good me trying to work in thousandths of an inch! I tried again and again to settle down – I had a pretty short fuse, and that alone lost me some jobs in my younger days. Before long I realised that there was only one place where I could be content.

By this time, Ralph had started his National Service, and the Skinners had gone. I was making my way towards Leighton Lock one afternoon when I became aware of boats behind me – after all, most marine engines were rather noisy! Except for the Gardners; I can remember one day during my early rambles sitting on a gate at Church lock and being blissfully unaware of approaching boats until a fore-end appeared under the bridge. It was the Beechey brothers, with their pair of Limited boats.

But now there was no mistaking the distinctive 'pomp – pomp – a – pomp' of a Bolinder as it slowed down. The boats reached the lock just as I did, and they turned out to be a Barlows pair with Ernie and Mable Wilson.

'Cooming fer a ride, chap?' Ern asked as he passed me a windlass. I rode with them as far as Fenny; after they'd headed off along the Fenny pound I was feeling a bit peckish, so I bought a pork pie from Fred Vaughan's shop and sat on the balance beam to eat it. Replenished, I was about to start walking up to Bletchley

Station when my attention was caught by the sound of a National engine, and as I looked back along the Fenny pound I saw a loaded pair approaching. They looked very smart in an unusual red and yellow livery, with their cratches covered.

As the motor came into the lock, I noticed the steerer. He looked, I thought, like quite a refined gent, and this was confirmed when in cultured tones he asked the very same question I'd had from Bill Humphries all that time ago:

'With boats?' I explained what I was doing there:

'No need to get a train – hop on and have a ride!' He went on to introduce the butty steerer as Jim Jackson, who had worked for the Grand Union company.

As we worked up from Talbot's Lock through Stoke Hammond Three, he told me the boats were his; I'd seen the name 'John Knill, Canal Carriers' signwritten on the cabinsides. He'd been a naval officer during the war, but having tried one or two business ventures, he'd seen these boats, the Columba and the Uranus, for sale; and he'd met Jim, almost by chance, who'd been able to show him the ropes. By now, I'd told him that I wasn't working:

'How would you like to come back on the canal?' was his response. Of course, I quickly said yes! 'Right – I'll come and talk to your parents.'

'I'm like a tortoise, I like to take my home with me!' he joked as I introduced him to my Mum and Dad: 'And this is Jim Jackson' he indicated his companion.

'Ah!' Dad piped up: 'I used to know a Jim Jackson.'

'That'd be my Dad!' Jim spoke up.

After a cup of tea, John, who was always known as 'Skipper', said to my parents:

'If young Fred wants to, we'll be glad to have him along.' And so off I went, on more canal adventures.

My home was to be the butty cabin. Jim occupied the motor's original cabin, while Skipper had a small cabin ahead of the engine-hole which a previous owner had had built there for his son – now Skipper used it as his office as well as his sleeping accommodation. True to naval tradition, Skipper kept a daily log! Something in the back of my mind was telling me I had seen these boats somewhere before; and then I remembered that some years earlier Ralph, Bob and I had found them tied at Brantom's Wharf – and we'd commented on the very dull overall green paintwork they'd been wearing at the time.

After some supper, Jim and Skipper departed for the motor while I settled in for the night. Next morning we ate breakfast, something Skipper always insisted on, and then set off. At Neal's Lock, we were met by the younger of my two elder brothers – he'd brought my shaving kit along with some extra clothes.

'Show your brother your skill on the tiller!' At Skipper's invitation, my brother rode on the gunwale as far as the road bridge where he'd left his motorcycle.

Our destination was Croxley – familiar territory! – which we reached that evening. We were lucky to get unloaded quite early the following morning, and once the boats were swept out and everything in its place we breasted up and moved off, getting on with other tasks like mopping off and brass-polishing, as only one was needed to steer. On the move, it was difficult to get at the brass porthole rims on the butty, because there is no gunwale below the cabin on a butty or a horse-boat, unlike a motor where the gunwale runs right along to the counter. We had a good road, with plenty of boats coming up, including one or two lighters with their beautiful horses, so I didn't need to go lock-wheeling.

Heading south from Croxley, I was on new ground. Or should that be new water? We passed through locks I had only ever heard of, including Denham, the deepest on the Grand Junction, close to the famous Denham film studios. I recall spotting a huge construction, painted a sky-blue colour – it was probably used in our dismal climate when the real sky wasn't as blue as the director required! Below Denham was Widewater Lock, so called because of the nearby reservoir.

As we progressed further south, the canal took on a more industrial look. After a few more locks, including Uxbridge and Coppermill, where a lot of the 'dry' coal went, we came to Cowley Lock and passed onto the Cowley pound which flowed into the

Paddington Arm. Eventually we arrived at the Bull's Bridge depot, past the drydocks and workshops to the lay-by where several pairs were tied by the stern to the concrete apron with their fore-ends facing out into the middle of the canal. They were a mixture of ex-Grand Union boats and Joshers (ex-F.M.C.).

Jim reversed ours up to the lay-by almost opposite the entrance to the Paddington Arm, and Skipper went off to report our arrival to the office. Although a number one, he was contracted to B.W.

Every so often, the tannoy would blare out "Steerer so-and-so, report to the office", and some boatman would scurry off for his orders. Then you would hear the clanking of a National, or the hiss of a Bolinder's blow-lamp, and after a while a pair of boats would ease out of the lay-by and head off, either down the arm or towards Brentford. We didn't get the call until the following morning, and so we had to spend the night in the lay-by; all night we could see the beacon from London's nearby airport.

Two pairs went off before us; then came the call:

'Steerer Knill, report to the office.' Skipper went off for the orders whilst Jim climbed down into the engine-hole. Even the two-cylinder oil engines of those days didn't have self-starters – each cylinder had to be primed using a special tool, then a hooked metal bar would be hung over the throttle cable so that its weight drew the cable tight and so partly opened the throttle, and finally the engine swung over with a detachable starting-handle, like an old-fashioned car engine. The National, as you will have gathered, had a cable in place of the mechanical linkage for the throttle, operated by a lever rather like a motorcycle brake lever; the gears were controlled by a big wheel with "ahead" and "astern" cast into it, with arrows indicating which way to turn the wheel for each direction.

Skipper came hurrying along:

'Brentford – Steel for Sampson Road.' Off we went, passing through the two locks at Norwood, known as Albert's Two – perhaps Albert had been a one-time lock-keeper there – and the descending the Hanwell flight, meeting both narrowboats and lighters coming up.

Brentford! What a sight for a newcomer! Boats and barges seemingly everywhere. Jim steered ours over to the far side of the very wide basin where warehouses and wharves stretched along the bank. The loading foreman said he'd get us loaded before dinner.

Now, the top cloths, except for those over the cratches, were folded and placed on the cabin-tops, but the planks were left in place. Bundles of long steel bars were gently lowered into the hold by a crane, where they were laid on baulks of timber so that the chains could be released. When the Columba was loaded – not up to the gunwales, with a heavy cargo like steel that would have been enough weight to sink the boat! – it was moved out and replaced by the Uranus. Jim and I set about sheeting up, drawing the side-cloths up into place and then unrolling the top-cloths along the planks and dropping them down over the side-cloths. The strings for the top-cloths had been stored rolled into one of the side-cloths – now they were thrown over the cloths, one end hooked onto rings on the gunwale on one side and the string passed through the ring on the other gunwale. To tie them off, we had to kneel on the planks and edge our way along from one to the next.

As soon as the butty was ready and the tickets handed over, we set off back up the canal, stopping overnight at Boxmoor where we refreshed ourselves in the Fishery Inn. Then, as usual, it was time for supper – cheese and pickles with bread and butter, washed down with a mug of that wonderful tea.

Chapter Five

The Brummagem Road

Early morning, a quick wash and breakfast – bacon and eggs, bought from a canal-side shop and stored in a cupboard in the butty's stern. That day, I did quite a bit of steering on both boats, as well as seeing to that dratted swing-bridge at Winkwell; the night saw us at Fenny Stratford.

The following day was a long one, bringing us through Braunston and onto the southern Oxford Canal, to the point where "yeh tairns off fer Brummagem". A massive bridge carries the towpath over the junction, another path turning underneath it, and some way along we came to three downhill locks, the like of which I had never seen before. There were no gate paddles at all, just four big ground paddles, one at each corner of the lock, and these were heavy structures encased in metal posts which for some unexplained reason all lean slightly away from the lockside. A squared end of the gearing, where your windlass fitted, protruded from a central part of the casing and was secured in the up position by a clip and a chain. These were Calcutt Locks, which the boaters referred to as 'Wigrams'.

All of the locks we met that day were of the same pattern – a flight at Southam, where we saw a number of boats loading at the cement works, then Long Itchington and so down to the floor of the Avon valley. We finally ended the day at Leamington Spa. The brother I mentioned earlier was then courting a girl from that town

– they were married later – and, being Saturday, I knew he would be there. He'd told me that her street backed onto the canal, so I took it into my head to go and give them a surprise. But in spite of searching for ages and asking the locals, I never did find the place!

Sunday morning dawned, and after breakfast we got under way, passing through the two locks at Warwick and on to Hatton Twenty-One. Some twerp apparently named these as the 'Stairway to Heaven'! More like the other place. At the top we spotted a group of bus-drivers taking their ease:

'Busman's holiday' said the Skipper with his usual dry wit! In fact, they had been bringing visitors to the nearby mental hospital. Jim saw the look of relief on my face as we cleared the last lock, and just said:

'There's another five.' There were indeed – at Knowle. All of these were big locks, of the same type as we had encountered the previous day. Between Hatton and Knowle lays Shrewley Tunnel – better known to the boaters as Hatton Tunnel, it is unique in having a separate narrow tunnel for the horses to pass through. I can imagine it in the days of horseboats, the handlers leading the horse through while the boat is legged through the main tunnel.

All the way through the locks on the Brummagem road I had been noticing what looked like derelict narrow chambers alongside the modern wide ones. I asked Skipper if they had actually been locks at some time, and he explained that this stretch had originally been built as two independent canals, the Warwick & Napton, and the Warwick & Birmingham. All of the locks had been narrow then – imagine working a pair through Hatton in those days! If you didn't meet boats coming the other way it would be like having to work a flight of 42... In 1929, Skipper went on, both had become part of the Grand Union system. The company had ambitions to work wide boats through to Birmingham, and these new wide locks were built to accommodate them, but the scheme never really took off.

By now we had passed Knowle and were travelling on the last pound, about ten miles according to Skipper. We were listening to a small battery radio which he had placed on the cabin-top; the programme was 'Down Your Way', a popular show of the day in which the presenter would interview a variety of people from a given area, and then each would choose a piece of music. The presenter then was Richard Dimbleby, and we shared a grin at one of the songs chosen: 'Cruising down the river on a Sunday afternoon...' Very appropriate!

Gradually we were drawing near to Birmingham, and I began to see why it was known as the Black Country. We passed soot-encrusted warehouses, and, despite it being Sunday, palls of black smoke hung in the sky before us. Much of the Industrial Revolution had centred on the Birmingham area, partly because of the number of coalfields surrounding it, seeing it grow from a little Warwickshire town into the great conurbation it is today.

Having reached Sampson Road depot, we drew into the dock and tied up – that's where the photograph on the cover of this book was taken. After cleaning up and having a meal, Skipper suggested we could all do with a bath. Not on board, of course! Many of the old back-to-back terraced houses of Birmingham still had no bathrooms, and the local council had for many years provided public bath-houses. We repaired to one such, and after refreshing ourselves outwardly, decided to refresh ourselves inwardly as well. Thus I was introduced to the pleasures of Flower's Midland Ale! After a drink or two, we returned to the boats for supper and bed.

Morning came, and with it preparations for unloading. The top cloths were untied and neatly folded, stacked out of the way to be stored under the cratches later. The side cloths were rolled down along the gunwales, the uprights and planks removed. Beneath each of the beams there was a chain which could be drawn tight, the idea being to prevent the sides of the boat from spreading. Unloading began, and once the butty was empty work began on the motor; when that too was finished we set off for our load of coal from Baddesley. Our route there was along the old boaters' 'Bottom Road' – out of Birmingham on the Birmingham & Fazeley Canal, running downhill to the junction with the Coventry Canal at Fazeley. Before the Grand Junction was built this was the original route into and out of Birmingham. But first we had to drop down the narrow locks of Camp Hill. The third lock down was very dark as it was crossed by both the road and railway – this lock has since been relocated, when they built the new bypass road.

In the basin below the flight, we turned towards Saltley and the end of the Grand Union Canal. Perhaps the best-known place on Birmingham's canals is Gas Street Basin – in those days it certainly lived up to its name! Even then, many houses and factories were lit by gas, the old 'Town Gas', produced by roasting coal in what were known as retort chambers. My parents lived near the gasworks in Leighton Buzzard and I can still recall seeing flames shooting high in the air from the furnaces. Town Gas had a very pungent smell. On our way we passed Saltley gasworks, where a Thomas Clayton boat was loading tar, a by-product of the production process. Scientists tell us that before the last ice-age Britain was sub-tropical, with dense tree growth, and this is why we have such extensive coalfields.

'We'll be lucky if we don't pick sommat up in the blades' was Jim's comment as we travelled through Saltley. That time, in fact, we were lucky, but it was a notorious area for rubbish in the cut – old rope fenders and bicycle tyres, which were the devil to get off the blades – chucking back would rarely shift stuff like that. But at last we began to climb into more pleasant scenery, and in time we arrived at Fazeley Junction where we turned onto the Coventry and began to make our way towards Atherstone and the Baddesley Colliery.

Once there, we loaded for Croxley and, having delivered our load, went on to Bull's Bridge where we were to leave the butty for some repairs. In no time we were heading for Birmingham with just the Columba; now we had only the one boat, Jim and I had to share the motor's cabin. Skipper let me steer through Blisworth Tunnel!

Once that trip was over, the butty was ready for us and we were back to normal working. But this journey was still to be rather different – Skipper had been asked to collect an old boat from the Wendover Arm, just above Marsworth top lock, which turned out to be an old Harvey-Taylor motor by the name of the Queen. It was engineless and sat high out of the water like an empty butty, and the tiller was missing, so steering would have to be done using only the ram's head. On a motor boat, the prop-wash working on the rudder does much of the steering – no engine, no prop-wash! We put a snatcher on the fore-end, running to the stern of our butty; the Queen had to go to Barlow's yard in Braunston.

With three boats, each lock had to be worked twice. The tunnels were quite a problem too, as all I had to guide me was what we called a 'monkey' light, a small electric lamp placed on the cabin-top. You won't need to guess who got that job. But thankfully we reached Braunston without incident, and then continued our journey.

After unloading at Sampson Road, Skipper came back to the boats:

'Chocolate!'

'Thank you' I said, thinking he had a treat for us.

'No – we're going to *load* chocolate!' And off we went, through the heart of the city and so to the Cadbury Brothers factory at Bournville.

The chocolate was in large slabs, covered in sacking. Jim, Skipper and I were in the boats whilst the men on the wharf wheeled the load out from the warehouse on sack-barrows. There with us were one or two of Cadbury's own boats, loading cases of chocolate bars or unloading milk-churns.

When our boats were loaded, we moved back up the canal a way. Skipper and Jim wanted to go for a drink, but as this was a special cargo, I was left 'on guard'. As I've already said, I get rather jumpy at night, and having earlier noticed a suspicious-looking character hanging around, I fetched Skipper's twenty-bore shotgun and a couple of cartridges from his cabin. Mind you, what I'd have done if anyone actually tried to get on board, I don't know! In the event, I returned them to their place shortly before the other two came back, and never said a word about borrowing them.

At daybreak, having breakfasted, we began to make our way back onto the Grand Union and in just over two days reached our destination at Hayes in Middlesex. Our next trip was the almost obligatory load of steel to Sampson Road, and then coal again from Newdigate colliery near Bedworth, where we arrived around mid-day on the Saturday. There would be no chance of loading until the Monday morning, but as there were no other boats there at least we would be first. Still there, having just loaded, were Bill and Rose Whitlock's Samuel Barlow pair. Bill had now got Jack Skinner's old motor, the Kent – Jim and I joined him in the engine-hole as the Bolinder was heating up, and Jim had the honour of 'kicking off'.

Saturday afternoon was mostly spent on shopping for supplies, and in the evening we visited a very nice pub where I got in to conversation with a very lovely lady. Also in there were a number of retired ex-boatmen, among them Joe Bray senior, who I had known when he lived in Linslade. On our way back to the boats, Jim remarked to me:

'You twairp – 'er fancied you!'

'We wouldn't have minded!' Skipper put in.

'No fear!' said I: 'She might have been married, and I don't want to get a thick ear from some irate husband!'

Skipper was of the Roman Catholic faith, and the next morning he went off to church somewhere in Bedworth, as he would if we were tied up near a town on a Sunday. I later learned that he was the son of a baronet, and in fact succeeded to the title some years after I knew him. Jim and I spent our morning doing the domestic chores, sweeping out our cabins, cleaning the brasswork and getting the boats ready for loading. When Skipper returned, he set about cooking lunch; in the afternoon, we sat around reading the papers he had brought back from town with him. Monday morning, and after breakfast we started loading our coal, which was to go to Nash Mills near Hemel Hempstead.

Soon after that, I decided that I wanted to go back to Leighton Buzzard to find work, and so I left Jim and Skipper. Shortly after I left, Jim got married and went to live in Rugby; Skipper, I gather, went to work for Barlows as fleet manager, but later returned to his own business with a new mate – he and I were to meet again in the years to come.

Chapter Six

An Interlude

I have to admit here that again I found I couldn't settle to any of the jobs I was able to obtain and often ended up with time on my hands. As you might imagine, much of this time was spent around the canal, and as Ralph had now finished his National Service, for a time we resumed our old ways, wandering the towpath. We encountered George Beechey on his S.E.Barlow boats (the motor was the Union Jack), and Jim and Doris Collins.

During this period I again met up with George and Sonia Smith, and of course went for a ride with them. George asked if I would be interested in a boating job again; I said 'who with?', upon which Sonia told me that there was a man in Rickmansworth who had begun to operate holiday boats. If I was keen they would contact him for me? I said I would be very interested; and in due course a letter arrived, inviting me to go down and meet him.

The man's name turned out to be Michael Street; his wife was with him, and another lady by the name of Peggy. They had two old motor boats, both of which had been converted to carry passengers with small cabins in what had been the cargo holds separated by a central aisle. One boat was an old Josher whose name I cannot remember; the other was the last motor boat run by George Garsides, the Nancy, fitted with a twelve-horsepower Petter. I wasn't entirely happy with the arrangements, but as George and Sonia had gone to so much trouble to get the job for me, I felt

I had to give it a go. Michael and his wife shared one of the original cabins, and Peggy, who with Mrs Street did the catering, had one of the little passenger cabins. There was no more spare room, so I would have to sleep on the floor in a sleeping bag, which meant that I could not get to bed until all the passengers had retired for the night.

Whilst I was sussing out the engine the passengers began to arrive. The engine itself I was familiar with – it was the electrics which caused all the headaches. Michael had set up a dynamo which was driven from the flywheel, but this often blew the fuses which meant that the batteries weren't getting properly charged. I was leaning out of the engine-hole doors as a very nice lady came to join the boat:

'What do you call the engine?' she asked.

'Lots of things!' I replied. We chatted for a while; I used the boater's term 'Starn' for the stern of the boat, and she laughed and told me that her father was the captain of a fishing boat somewhere on the south coast, and he always referred to the 'starn'. She turned out to be a school-teacher; we got on very well, and she even invited me to spend a holiday with them, but other events got in the way and I never did get my holiday.

The Petter, like some other engines, could be awkward, and the Nancy's was no exception. When started by swinging the flywheel, it was supposed to rotate in one direction, but sometimes it would bounce back and start the wrong way. I had learned from Bill Humphries that the best way to correct this was to push down on the foot-lever which was used to stop the engine and wait until it was nearly stopped, and then give the lever a quick two or three pumps. It would usually then start to run the right way.

When the passengers had eaten and performed their necessary ablutions we set off, Michael steering while I lock-wheeled. Above Cassio Lock I came across a group of men wandering around on the towpath, all dressed in eighteenth-century costume. I stopped to ask what was going on, and one of them told me:

'We're making a film called 'The House in the Square'. See that couple over there? That's Patricia Medina and Tyrone Power!' They were well-known stars back then, Tyrone Power perhaps best known for starring in 'The Mark of Zorro'. The boat came into the lock, which caused a stir of interest among the film crew; Michael handed over the tiller to me.

We stopped at Hemel Hempstead and again at Berkhamstead for the passengers to explore the area around the canal. We finally ended up at Marsworth, where they went off to investigate the village, except for my school-teacher friend who stayed talking to me while I gave the engine a good clean-up with a rag soaked in diesel and checked the lubricators. By this time my bones were aching, and on the way down to Leighton I told Michael I didn't feel that I could go on. In any case, I was used to working boats, not to having to stop two or three times a day at the whim of the passengers.

I got a job with the local laundry then, as a van boy collecting and delivering around Leighton. It wasn't a bad sort of job on the whole, but I wasn't too happy at having to collect the money from the customers. One in particular was always ready to moan about everything, this wasn't right or that wasn't right; and, not feeling too good, I was a bit rude on occasion! She reported me, and so I packed it in. But one of our runs had been down to Berkhamstead, where the driver and I would stop for lunch in a cafe overlooking Broadwater Lock, which brought the old yearning back, so I wasn't sorry to leave!

Once more I was at a loose end, frequenting the towpath, meeting old friends and hitching rides on the boats.

Chapter Seven

The Skinners

One morning I was walking up to Grove Lock when I heard the rattle of a National. I waited to see who was coming, and got a bit of a surprise – it was Jack and Rose Skinner, who Ralph had worked with before, but now they were on a pair of British Waterways boats, old ex-Grand Union craft. After helping them through, I needed no second bidding to go for a ride with them, taking my turn at lock-wheeling and steering along the way. At one point Jack asked me to steer the butty so that Rose could see to her cooking – she was baking a meat pie of the kind which I remembered Ralph drooling over. You may be sure we all enjoyed some!

On reaching Boxmoor I was about to take my leave when Jack asked if I would like to work with them. I don't need to tell you what my reply was!

'Roit' said Jack, 'You go stiddy orf an' we'll go stiddy orf, an' we'll see you soon.'

The following day, having told my parents of my plans, I took my bike and set off to ride down to Croxley. I met several pairs heading north, but none were going the other way, so I just kept on riding. I arrived about three in the afternoon; Jack, still waiting to unload, was standing in the butty's hatches.

'Got the kettle on?' I called out to him; 'Ah!' came the reply.

Reaching the lock, I heaved the bike onto my shoulder and crossed the gates. Seeing all the other boats waiting there to empty,

I realised why I hadn't seen any going down! After many greetings from such as Charlie Littlemore who was now working with another chap, and Johnny Wilson, still with his mum and dad, I eventually reached Jack's boats. Having deposited my odds and sods into the motor cabin I climbed onto the butty, to be met with a superb stew and of course a mug of tea. The boat women all made full and wonderful use of the food they bought!

My new home was the motor 'Caldy'; the butty, if I remember right, was the 'Taplow' Many of the Grand Union boats were named after towns and cities – Caldy was somewhere in Scotland. I knew of two others whose names originated north of the border: Greenock and Stirling. Fellows, Morton & Clayton used a range of different names for their boats; I remember animal names like the Jaguar, Lion, Bison and Python. By the middle of the following day we were dealt with, and made our way to Bull's Bridge. Our orders, which came as no surprise, were for steel, but this time for Tyseley rather than Sampson Road.

Neither Jack nor Rose could read or write, and I was often asked to write letters to Rose's parents at Banbury, a task which Ralph had also undertaken while he was working with them. From Tyseley we loaded from Baddesley with coal for Nash Mills, where it was unloaded by a very ancient steam crane which ran on rails. This pattern of steel followed by coal was repeated a few times, but then we had a change – this was wheat for a mill on the River Nene.

The arm to Northampton turns off from the Grand Junction, as some readers will know, at Gayton on the Blisworth pound. As a child I had often seen it from the train, as the railway line through Roade runs close to it – and here I was, actually travelling on it. At the mill, our load was drawn out by suction, which made our lives a bit easier.

After emptying we made our way back up to the main line of the canal and headed north for Buckby and Braunston, where we stopped. At Sutton's the next day, we were ordered to load at Newdigate for Croxley.

It was whilst waiting there that I saw Jack chatting with an old chap by the bridge, where there were a couple of cottages. When he came back, he said to me:

'That were 'Enry Wenlock – you 'eerd about 'is gel?' I had indeed – Bill Garner at Hammond Three had told Ralph and I once. The Wenlocks had worked for the Limited, with the Sarah and the famous (thanks to that film!) Sunny Valley. According to Bill, the boats had been going up the locks loaded; Alice was steering the motor, and as she set back to pick up the tow, she slipped the tiller string on before putting the engine into reverse. But as she stood up after attaching the towrope, it broke, the tiller came sweeping around and knocked her into the water.

Seeing what had happened, her dad rushed along the butty's planks to stop the boat, which was now reversing slowly into the lock. But Alice was trapped between the motor's stern and the butty fore-end – she was crushed, and badly cut about by the propeller. Bill helped to separate the boats and lift Alice's body from the water; then he telephoned the Linslade police and called for a doctor. Once the coroner had deliberated, Alice was interred in Old Linslade churchyard; her devastated parents left the cut.

Jack went on:

'Arter 'er was killed, some chap writ a poem about 'er. 'Enry arxed if you would read it fer 'im?'

'Of course!' I replied, 'does Mrs Wenlock want to hear it too?'

'Nah – 'Er can't abide to 'ear it as it upsets 'er.'

That evening Henry came over with his precious possession. Once we had all seated ourselves around the butty's stern I began to read – I don't remember much of it; the gist was about what she had meant to her family and friends. The closing line was:

"In Heaven I am Alice still."

After a moment of silence, Jack said quietly:

'That's all true, ain't it.' Henry thanked me profusely before making his way home.

Among the letters I had written for Rose was one inviting her parents to join them for a trip. Duly we picked them up at Sutton's, where a friend had brought them. Things were a bit crowded! Mr Hone, Jack and I shared the motor cabin while his wife shared the butty with Rose and little Joyce, their daughter. They did the whole trip with us, and I was intrigued by Mr Hone's stories about the old days of horse-boating:

'Ah, you moit think boatin's 'ard now, but 'oss-boatin' were much 'arder!'

My father had worked horses so I knew a little about such things; I asked him about those on the canals feeding on the move, and the risk of them getting colic as a result:

'Ah' he said 'We didn't let 'em feed too long – per'aps on a flight o' locks or a short pound. If we 'ad toime we'd feed 'em afore settin' orf.'

At the end of that trip we dropped Mr and Mrs Hone off at Sutton's and headed straight on to Baddesley Colliery to load for Croxley. Jack rather broke the rules at one point on this trip! The lock at Fenny Stratford is very shallow, only about twelve inches, and as we approached we could see that the lock was empty, with the bottom gates standing open. I was on the Caldy with Jack:

''Old toit mate!' he said, and aimed through the lock at the centre of the top gates, winding the engine up to full throttle. Bang! Dead centre – the gates sprang apart and in an instant both boats were through into the Water Eaton pound and heading for Talbot's Lock. There was a lengthsman who lived at Fenny, and no doubt he heard the crash, but in the dark would have no idea who was responsible – just as well! This sort of thing had been done before, and could be punishable by a heavy fine or even dismissal. That night we stopped at Leighton. After emptying and reaching Bull's Bridge we had orders for another load of wheat for Northampton; and after unloading that, we stopped overnight at Braunston, setting off for Sutton's the next morning.

Jack and Rose had a nice old dog called Gyp, and many times while waiting to load or empty I would take Gyp and young Joyce for a walk so that Rose could get on with her other chores. This day, as we were getting along the northern Oxford, Jack called from the butty's fore-end:

'Syn Gyp?' I called back from the motor's tiller:

'I thought he was on the butty, or on the bank?' Sometimes he would run alongside the boats on the towpath, stopping to sniff about as any dog will, but always catching up with us. But now there was no sign of him:

'Oi'll tek the boike an'go an' look for 'un' said Jack; he grabbed the bike and pedalled off back the way we had come. We were almost at Hillmorton before he came puffing along:

'Nary a sign of 'un. Oi'm boogered eff Oi knows where 'e is!'

I had just run Caldy into the full lock; I went into the cabin for something, and from the bed-hole came a scratching and a whining. I quickly dropped the bed down, and out jumped Gyp! Poor old thing, he'd been there all that time! I knew what had happened – another habit of his was to leap through the doorway into my cabin in the mornings when Jack came over to call me. He would get on my bed whilst I dressed, and he had done so that morning, as usual. But this time, when I left the cabin I hadn't seen him curled up at the foot of the bed, and must have thought he had already got out. So I closed the bed and shut him in!

'Where were 'e?' Jack asked, cussing and fussing him at the same time. I explained, and he laughed: 'Sairves 'im roit!' With that crisis over, we went on our way.

After our next coal run we had two short trips up to Nash Mills with wood pulp from Brentford. On one of them, Alf Bodley had gone ahead of us, and that gave my mate Freddie, his young son, and I the chance to get together for a while. We emptied where once Dickinson's own boats used to bring rags – they had then run at least one steamer.

Then back to Bull's Bridge, where a different run was in the offing.

Chapter Eight

Robin Hood Country

Jack came scurrying along the lay-by:

'Branford – Fruit fer Not'nam!'

So we were off again for Brentford, where we loaded canned fruit, which came in crates. This had to be loaded carefully, and then fully covered.

It was on the Braunston summit, not far from Buckby top lock, that a right turn at Norton Junction put us on the Leicester Section of the Grand Union Canal, which was also made up of two of the original privately-owned canals. This southern section was the first 'Grand Union' Canal, cut to join the older Leicester and Northampton Union Canal to the Grand Junction and thence to London.

The first locks we met were at Watford (a little Northamptonshire village, not the other one!). The locks on this stretch are all narrow, and mostly concentrated into staircases, where the top gate of one lock forms the bottom gate of the next and the boats go from one chamber straight into the next. Getting the motor through is easy, of course, but the butty then has to be bow-hauled, a job made a lot more difficult because these locks have little wooden footbridges over each lock-tail which get in the way of the tow-rope. We were being buttied here by a young chap named Sam Horne, taking timber to Leicester with his wife – Sam had once worked as mate for Jack and Rose.

Above Watford lies the twenty-mile summit, which takes in Crick Tunnel. It's quite a pleasant stretch, but does meander somewhat! Then there's Husbands Bosworth Tunnel, close to where Richard the Third was defeated. At last we reached Foxton, where two staircases of five locks (narrow again, with those blessed bridges) descend to join the Leicester and Northampton Union Canal. An arm (part of the old canal) goes off to Market Harborough, but we turned left for Leicester – the locks from here are wide, and Jack called them the 'old 'uns', and there's another tunnel, at Saddington. Very soon we arrived at Leicester, where Sam was to unload, and we tied for the night. In the morning, we set off down more locks until we arrived at Trent Lock, where we were met by the river pilot who was to take our now-breasted boats up to the wharf.

Not long after arriving a big steam barge in BW livery moored astern of us, dwarfing our boats. Looking out through the open doors of Caldy's cabin, I noticed a young lad peering intently at the rose and castle decoration on the door panels. I went out to speak to him; in a broad east midland accent, he asked:

'Do yer paint 'em y'sens?'

'No' I answered, 'they're done at our depot in London.'

'Loondon!' he exclaimed: 'Loondon!' We might as well have just come from America! The barge captain, who turned out to be his father, had just emerged, and the lad called to him, still excited:

'Ay Dad, them from Loondon!'

'Oh aye' came the reply – no doubt Dad had seen boats from 'Loondon' many times before.

I was invited aboard for a cup of tea – this time with real milk. The crew consisted of the captain and his wife, another chap who was the mate, and the young lad. We had all arrived on a Saturday afternoon, so the rest of the day was spent quietly. On Sunday, Jack and I did a bit of tidying up, and found ourselves a 'watering hole'.

Next day we emptied, and then set off, still breasted, Jack steering, further down river until we reached the junction with the Trent and Mersey Canal, where we met a lot of other boats, many of them Joeys. Eventually, we came to Fradley where the Trent and Mersey joins up with the Coventry Canal – Jack's parents were tied opposite the White Swan Inn, and we all spent a pleasant hour or two in the pub garden.

Orders had been forwarded for us to load at Baddesley for Croxley, after which we did a run with steel for Sampson Road. On this trip we arrived at Buckby bottom lock (or Whilton if you prefer!) quite late; Charlie MacDonald, Sid's brother, was there, and called across to Jack:

'You comin' for a drink?'

'Ah' Jack replied, 'Just now.' (Which translates as 'later'). The Nixons were there too, and one or two others. About this time, Joseph Stalin was having one of his purges in Russia – Charlie, an avid reader, was talking about this, and Jack said, in almost hushed tones:

'Eff theers a God, Whoy don't 'E stroike 'im dead one of these dark noits?'

'Quoite roit!' came another voice.

We left the Spotted Cow some time later, a little the worse for wear – having put the world in general and Russia in particular to rights, we went our separate ways.

Our next journey from Brentford was steel again, for Sampson Road, where there was a strike by the men on the wharf which meant that it might be some time before we could unload. But BW found work for us at Cadbury's unloading the milk boats, as the men there were on strike as well – it was all part of a National dock strike. Each morning a lorry would pick us up to take us to Bournville, and bring us back around five o'clock – there were four or five pairs waiting. It was during this period that Jack and I paid a visit to the Birmingham Hippodrome, where the late great Max Wall was appearing. Eventually the problem was resolved, and normal working was resumed.

Our next coal run was to Nash Mills. Whilst we were there, both the Beecheys and the Granthams passed, on their way to Home Park – this wasn't George and Albert Beechey now, but George and Liz (nee Grantham); George's motor was S.E.Barlow's Union Jack. Ernie Grantham was now married too, and working for BW, so the Grantham boats were crewed by Joe and his mother. Jack suggested I go and lend a hand, which I did, earning myself a few shillings into the bargain. I'd thought one pair was enough to empty by hand, but two! 104 tons of large coal! We all mucked in, even Liz and her mum. Going back up, I steered George's boats – but not for the first time, as I'd ridden with him once soon after he was married.

Two more steel runs were followed by another trip with wood pulp to Nash. Whilst there, we learned from southbound boaters about a mini-tornado which had struck the Leighton Buzzard area, so I came home during the evening to check that my folks were all right. A lot of damage had been done, but thankfully their end of the town had been untouched. Also during my time with Jack and Rose, my afore-mentioned brother got married, so I had to take a little time off to go to Leamington Spa, spending two nights at my parent's home. I caught up with Jack again at Croxley, but this time I was able to ride with boats rather than having to cycle as I had the last time!

Jack was a bit of a dour type of chap who rarely smiled, but he taught me well, letting me do most of the steering on Caldy. But all the same, he was generous, and always ready to treat me to a drink. Rose, on the other hand, was always friendly, and would occasionally sit in my cabin with me and chat, or ask me to write a letter to her folks. She would talk about when she and her sister Betty were young, and working with their parents – one of Mr Hone's boats was named after his daughters. For a long time, whatever butty Jack had, they had the tail from one of her dad's horses attached to the ram's head – this was quite a tradition from the days of horse-boats. If a favourite horse had died, often its tail would be hung from the ram's head.

Another tradition related to the chain used to fasten the cabin doors when you were away from the boat. The chain was attached to the slide, a large wooden panel on runners, which covered the upper hatch opening above the doors – with everything closed, the chain would be padlocked to a staple on one door. It was considered real bad luck to let the chain hang down during the day, just why I was never able to establish! I've mentioned the water cans, kept by the chimney with the mop through the handles; the handbowl, the boater's equivalent of a sink, was placed against the side of the table-cupboard. Personal hygiene was carried out whenever possible – always after loading or emptying. This also involved keeping the children clean, and giving the men time to shave. I found a very good barber in Brentford!

Of course it wasn't all work and no play. Many a time whilst at Sutton's waiting to load, a number of boaters would gather in the Greyhound, or on a Saturday the younger ones among us would go into Coventry, to go to the pictures or to look for girls. At Croxley, we would run about with some of the boat girls in the rag sheds. I recall Charlie Littlemore, Johnny Wilson and myself, once when our boats were tied below Marsworth bottom lock, getting the bus into Leighton Buzzard – but as this was the only bus, and the blessed thing started back again after half-an-hour, we had the choice of going straight back or facing a damned long walk!

And so time was marching on. Soon it would be time to leave, as within a month or two I was due to join the army – it was towards the end of the summer that year, 1951, that I left Jack, after a trip with grain to the buffer depot on Tring summit.

Chapter Nine

Egyptian Sojourn

After leaving Jack, to fill in some time I obtained work with a second-hand car company in Leighton. This entailed rubbing down the paintwork ready for respraying – to do this we used emery paper and buckets of cold water. And to add insult to injury they sent me to the firm's small yard in Linslade, which meant that at lunchtime it took me twenty minutes to walk home and another twenty minutes to walk back, which left me just ten minutes to eat my lunch, which thankfully was always ready.

So I wound up at a loose end again, and started to wander the towpath. But now some familiar faces were beginning to disappear from the scene. Many younger boaters were beginning to think that life on the bank would be better – the hours were regular, and if you could get a job somewhere like a car factory you could earn the grand sum of twenty pounds a week. It doesn't sound like much these days, but back then it was great – it might take the average boatman a month to earn that much. Of course they hadn't reckoned with things like rent or income tax, which those of us who lived on the bank took for granted. However, many did stay on the boats, as they knew no other way of life.

Needless to say, I made use of this period. On one occasion, I met up with a couple I hadn't met before, who worked for BW. They offered me a job, and I was only too pleased to go along. It was okay for a while, but when we arrived at Bull's Bridge things changed – up until then, they had been very nice to me, but now they had to put the motor on the dry dock. I wasn't asked to join them on the butty in the evenings, and so early on the second day I sneaked out of the cabin, took my bike and left the depot.

By mistake, I turned in the wrong direction and found myself on the Great West Road. Snow and ice lay everywhere, and I was forced to push my bike instead of attempting to ride it; however, I derived some amusement from watching a taxi twirl around in a manner that any ice dancer would have envied. The scene began to look familiar, and suddenly I realized I was looking down on the basin at Brentford, where the only boats I could see were two motors, being sheeted up. I walked down to them and instantly recognized the red and yellow livery that one boat carried – the other was in BW's blue and yellow, but both bore the legend 'John Knill London' on the cabin-sides.

'Where have you sprung from?' Skipper asked in amazement; I told him what had happened.

'Come aboard, we're just going to eat' was the reply. Skipper introduced his companion – sad to say my memory is slipping, but I think it could have been Tom Foxon.

Having eaten, we set off through the ice passing big barges covered in ice above Albert's Two. Skipper thought it might be best if I stayed in the cabin until we'd passed Bull's Bridge. As we headed into Hayes, he said that he had some business to attend to in London, and would I take the Columba? He would meet us in a few days.

We pushed on as best we could, despite ice collecting behind the gates at every lock. The worst was behind the top gates, and of course we were working uphill – at lock 80 we tried everything, using the rake and our shafts, to no avail. I suggested ramming the gates, charging them at full throttle, and after two attempts it worked. From then on it wasn't so bad – boats ahead had done a lot to make the road easier for us. We decided to tie up at Hunton Bridge, having had enough for one day. We got a meal together between us, and sat talking for an hour or so before retiring for the night.

I woke first the next morning, and went over to the other boat, which Skipper had named Kenelm:

'Are you ready for some breakfast?' I asked; the reply was that he'd be over after having a wash, so I thought it as well to attend to my own ablutions first. Having had our eggs and bacon, and of course a mug of strong tea, we got the engines started and began to creep up the cut again. Skipper met us at Wolverton, where I got off and made my way to the station and home. During this time not only did I meet up with Skipper, but also Alec Purcell, who was on his way to Wellingborough with wheat. I went along with him, returning from Northampton the next day.

I managed to get a job at the local sand quarries, but still kept going down the towpath at the weekends. Rather like the old days, except that there was no Ralph or Bob. It was good to meet up with people like Ben Nixon, and Joe Bray junior, who was now married. I also came across a young couple who were strangers to me – she was off the bank, but he came from a boating family who had worked up north. They'd only just started working the Junction, and he asked me if I would like to work with them, but sadly I had to tell them I would soon be going into the army; they were a very nice couple – she called him Josh, I remember.

This wasn't the only offer I had at that time: In the past, both Jim Collins and Bill Whitlock had asked if I would join them, although Jim then had his mother-in-law with them – he'd always said that when she was gone, he and Doris would take me on. Now Mrs Grantham (not the same one I mentioned in the last chapter!) had left them, but it was too late.

Eventually it was time to register for my army service. I had decided to volunteer for the regular army rather than wait to be called up for National Service, and was sent to join the Royal Engineers at Great Malvern in Worcestershire.

On my way from Paddington I caught a glimpse of the canal at West Drayton – I had often seen trains along there on a high embankment. Most had been in Great Western livery, although for over three years now they had been combined with the Southern, the London & North Eastern and London, Midland &

Scottish companies in the nationalized British Railways. My train also passed through Oxford – a place I had never been to, even on the cut, and to be honest had never expected to.

After my basic training I was posted to Aldershot where I trained as a driver. During that period I spent a lot of my spare time walking the towpath of the nearby Basingstoke Canal, but never saw any boats – the Basingstoke had not been used for commercial traffic for many years even then. In the summer of 1952, along with others from the training camp, I was posted to a field regiment in Egypt.

Chapter Ten

Jack Munk

In 1954, after almost three years service, I was home at last. For the first month I was on de-mob leave, technically still in the payroll of the army, and in that time I began to look for work in the transport industry. I thought then that my future, at least as far as work was concerned, was set – I'd been driving for over four years and had made up my mind to pursue that kind of job.

In the same road where my parents lived there was a small haulage firm. I had known the owner ever since I was a young boy because his yard was adjacent to the small farmyard which my father used, and he took me on, but only on trial because army driving was vastly different from civilian work. For one thing, most of my time had been on petrol-engined lorries (or trucks, as our American friends called them). Ex-service drivers in those days were given a certificate on leaving which could be exchanged for a civilian driving licence – not like today! The licence I received from Bedfordshire County Council, to whom the fees and road tax were payable then, allowed me to drive vehicles I had never been trained on. The lorry I was given was a four-wheeler with a Gardner four-cylinder diesel engine. A lot of truck and bus builders then used Gardners – the only trouble was that they were governed to prevent speeding, and also had a very slow gearchange, so it took me a while to get used to it. It had come from a nearby cement works, and by the end of the first day I was plastered!

This was only a temporary job – I'd been taken on mainly to cover holiday periods – and so before long I found myself at a loose end once more. I tried other haulage firms, but it was either "we'll let you know" or involved staying away overnight, which I wasn't prepared to do. And so it was that I started visiting the canals again, not really intending to go boating full-time but only to earn myself a few bob where I could by helping out.

It was on one of these casual visits that I met Jack Munk. I was talking to Arthur Morris, an ex-boater who had taken over as lock-keeper at Leighton when Mr Bambrook retired, when we heard the unmistakeable sound of a Bolinder approaching from somewhere near the Globe Inn. As they rounded the turn below the lock I saw that they were in a kind of reverse of the old Fellows, Morton & Clayton livery, with green panels and red borders.

The steerer on the motor, a tallish man with a rather weather-beaten face, murmured 'thanks' as I closed the gate for him. His companion, a shorter, swarthy chap, had strapped the butty in, and now both of them walked to the top end to attend to the paddles. I was gazing into the engine-hole when the motor steerer spoke:

'Ever sin one o' them afore?' he asked. I replied that I had been boating before going on army service, and was invited to go along with them for a ride, as far as Boxmoor. The captain introduced himself as Jack Munk, and his mate as Jimpty; he went on to tell me that he had worked for Harvey-Taylors before the war. I told him about the time when Skipper, Jim and I had taken the old Queen to Braunston:

'Well!' he exclaimed 'That were my ol' motor!' Then he said: 'I 'spec you know my brother 'Arry what works for the Limited?' Of course I did know Harry and his family; and two other friends, Jim Jackson and young Joe Bray had both married into the Munk family.

He asked if I would like to steer along the two-mile, which of course I was delighted to do. As we approached Neal's Lock at Slapton, I slowed down, put the engine onto reverse and then when we had stopped put it back to forward again. Jack looked surprised:

'Know a bit abaht it then' he said, and I told him about my

trips with Ernie Wilson, and the time I had taken Bill Hough's Lion round the Fenny pound.

'Well Oi'm blowed!' he said, 'this used ter be the Lion!' He explained that Willow Wren, the company he was working for, had bought some ex-Joshers from British Waterways – they'd renamed this boat the Bittern. I stayed with them to Boxmoor, helping out along the way (including that swingbridge at Winkwell); Jack asked where I lived in Leighton, and then gave me two pounds. I walked up to Hemel station to get my train home.

I still hadn't thought seriously about going back to full-time boating, but fate once more took a hand. I had been out with some mates one evening, about a week later; when I got home, my Dad said:

'The boaters have been looking for you.' When I asked who, he said that I had met them a week earlier, and if I wanted to go I had to meet them that night.

'Oi'm afraid you'll 'ave to share wi' me' Jack said as I stepped onto the butty, and I replied that I didn't mind:

'Where are we going?' I asked, and his answer came:

'Sam'son Road wi' steel.' In the words of a well-known comedian of the day, I might have known!

So it was next morning that we set off about five-thirty – Jack wanted to get a head start. I quickly learnt that Jack and Jimpty were both early birds! It was good to hear that old Bolinder pop-popping away – they had a sound that was rather hollow, and very distinctive. By mid-morning we were working up Stoke; Jack took the motor through both tunnels, but my turn was to come later. Buckby was soon behind us, and by afternoon we had gone down Braunston and onto the south Oxford heading for Napton and Wigrams where we tied for the night.

The next day saw us at Sampson Road by late in the afternoon. It was just as I had last seen it – we were the only boats there, and so got unloaded after a night's rest. That night I found out a bit more about Jack – mostly from Jimpty. It seemed he had been married, and had a son – some of his former brothers-in-law worked as loaders at Griff, and as Jack himself told me later:

'Them booggers don't talk to me an' Oi don't talk to them.' Jack also told me that he had been to sea at one time. I found him a pleasant chap, but he was always inclined, when we tied up, to go off on his own; there was one occasion when the three of us went for a drink together – but I'll come to that later! On the other hand, whenever I was with him, he was always ready to listen, and answer any questions I had. He showed me a pair of model boats that he had.

There wasn't much that Jack didn't know about Bolinders, although he had been brought up on horse-boats. For instance, he would remove the pigeon-box, which is a kind of skylight over the engine-hole, and attach two strings to the fuel pumps. Then, leaving the clutch in so that the propeller was always turning, he would use them to set the engine ahead or astern. I'd never seen this done before!

After emptying, it was as usual a case of going on the bottom road. The City Corporation's joey boats were still where I had seen them years before, and sadly the area down to Saltley hadn't changed much either. We had orders to load at Griff for Croxley. Lock-wheeling, at the second lock I found a Clayton's motor about to enter, coming the other way – to my surprise, the steerer was Charlie Roberts, who I had known when he worked for the Limited.

Now the dirt and grime was being left behind. Jack let me steer the Bittern, and it seemed no time at all before we were going up Atherstone locks and onto the long pound. We turned the boats towards that low bridge, but got away without having to dismantle the cratches. We were too late to load that day, and so had to stay overnight. Jimpty had relatives in Bedworth, so he set off to visit them, and Jack and I went our separate ways. I found the local watering-hole, but only stayed for one drink before returning to the boats where I made a pot of tea.

Jack came back later, looking smug:

'Oi've just been wi' a woman!' he said with a grin.

'Lucky bugger!' was my retort.

After supper, we retired, but later we heard Jimpty entering the motor's cabin.

We got loaded the next morning, behind Alf Best, who was now working for Willow Wren as well; and I discovered that Jack Skinner was also with them now. His motor was an odd one – although it was an ex-Grand Union boat, it had a Bolinder, which must have replaced the original National or Russell Newbery at some time. The GU motors didn't have a connecting door from the cabin into the engine-hole; and that door could come in very useful on a Bolinder boat, because it allowed the steerer to get into the engine-hole quickly if the engine stopped when you tried to reverse it, as they did sometimes.

After loading, we worked up to Braunston. Jack (Munk) always believed in getting as far as possible in the day – just as we thought about tying up, he'd say:

'D'yer mind if we go a bit fairther?'

At that time, lock-keepers were under orders to lock up at six o'clock. This was done by padlocking a chain around the handrails of the top gates of the top lock, and the bottom gates of the bottom lock of a flight.

From Braunston we made Marsworth – I had hoped for a stop in Leighton – and we were at Croxley by late afternoon the next day, where we found Alf laying just ahead of us. When we had settled down, it occurred to me that I hadn't seen the Bodley's on our travels, so I asked Jack about them:

'Yer won't see 'em any more, they'm finished' he told me. He went on: 'Young Freddie were killed, goin' down Sweeps Two. He were workin' a single motor, with 'is mam and dad buttyin' 'im. Any road, Alf were lock-wheelin', got ter the top o' the two, see the boat but no sign o' Fred. Arter callin' 'is name, Alf jumped down, the boat moved an' up come Freddie's body.' No-one knew whether Freddie had slipped on the wet lock-side, or lost his footing jumping down onto the cabin-top. With a single motor in wide locks, the boat can sometimes cross-wind, leaving the fore-end in one corner and the stern in the opposite one, which makes getting down onto the boat very tricky.

After Croxley it was down to Bull's Bridge, where Jack received orders for another load of steel for Birmingham, this time for Tyseley Wharf. And thence to Griff again, to load for the Nestlé plant at Hayes. Two more steel runs followed, both to Sampson Road, with coal to Croxley in between. And then we had a change of cargo – timber, for Tipton, in Staffordshire.

For this we had to go to Brentford, but this time the boats had to be taken through the two gauging locks onto part of the river – these locks were worked only by the lock-keepers, with big wheel-operated gates and paddles. The timber had been brought up from the docks by lighter, and was transferred direct onto the boats; once loaded, the top planks except for the foremost ones were laid on top of the timber, and the side and top cloths tied over them. Timber tended to make the boats light loaded, and therefore riding high in the water.

Once out of Albert's Two and onto the Cowley pound, where the cut is wider and deeper than most places, Jack said:

'Go an' pull the bracket up.' Bolinder engines have a lever on one side, which could give you extra speed – I went down into the engine-hole and moved the lever, which being on a ratchet rather resembled the handbrake of an old-fashion lorry.

On this journey we did stop at Leighton (or more correctly, Linslade), but we weren't tying up. In those days there was a small petrol station by Leighton Bridge, which also had a diesel pump by the canal where boats could refuel – it was closed later when the local council decided it was a hazard. After a short stop we were soon on our way again, stopping for the night below Stoke. The next night we tied above Warwick Two, just ahead of two holiday boats, and I was surprised to find that two of the girls working on them came from Linslade. I introduced myself, and we had quite a pleasant chat together. Then early off through Hatton and on to Knowle.

In earlier times, we would have turned off at Kingswood and followed the Stratford Canal, and then the Worcester and Birmingham, but we weren't allowed to use it then. That meant going on to join the bottom road at Aston, and up Farmer's Bridge locks. There were a number of Clayton's boats about, many of them horse-drawn plus a few single motors, although I don't recall seeing Charlie Roberts again. It was up near Walsall that I saw something I'll never forget as long as I live: A vast cemetery, stretching as far as I could see, coming down almost to the towpath – Jack said it was where victims of the bombing had been buried after the terrible pounding of Birmingham and Coventry during the war.

We eventually arrived at the timber yard where we were to deliver our cargo, which was unloaded by crane. There was a time when timber had been one of the chief cargoes on the canal; I recall a timber yard below Croxley lock, and another at Berkamstead which up until the 1940s was served by barges and narrowboats. There used to be a long-established timber merchants beside Bridge Street, the Linslade to Leighton Buzzard road (nowadays known as Leighton Road), and a big gate on the towpath close to the former railway bridge – I have often wondered if at one time timber might have been brought there by boat, but have never been able to find out for sure despite enquiring of some of the older boatmen.

'Where to now?' I asked Jack once everything was clean and tidy.

'Cannock Chase' was his reply – a place I had heard of but never been. We were there by the afternoon, and pulled into a small basin alongside a railway track, just by the Watling Street.

'Get some coal in mate' said Jack, adding 'from the cut.' Taking the ice rake, I began dredging around until I had enough to fill both cabin coal boxes. A lot of joeys loaded there – they always tended to load until well down in the water, and having no cloths, quite a bit of coal ended up in the canal. That evening all three of us sat in the butty's stern, talking until late.

'What d'yer reckon to it?' Jimpty asked; I replied that I had enjoyed the trip very much.

Having loaded the next day, we set off, making our way back into Birmingham, passing empty joeys on their way to load where we had just come from. Once in the city we were amongst blackened factories, some still working, some lying derelict; many of them were iron foundries, and I recall seeing joey boats being unloaded by hand. There was one factory which was different, and sticks in my memory – this was the famous Birmingham Small Arms company. Originally a gunsmiths, I'm sure that to everyone

B.S.A. is better known for their bicycles and motor cycles – a brand new one roared over a nearby bridge, obviously on test.

Another thing I remember from Birmingham is the high bridges, with doors set in their parapets for the benefit of the city fire brigade. Soon we began to climb locks until we came to Camp Hill, and so back onto the Grand Union. Jack proposed going on to Warwick, and Jimpty and I agreed – well, it was better than facing Hatton first thing in the morning!

Our load was for Nestlé's once more, but this time we had no back-load and so were empty boating to Sutton's. Just as well too! Jack had been asked to pick up an old butty from the limited's yard in Braunston and take it to S.E.Barlow's yard at Glascote. This time it wasn't too bad with three boats – an empty butty is much easier to handle than a dead motor, and we only had to work them all through Hillmorton and the stop-lock at Sutton's anyway.

At Bedworth, Jimpty did his usual disappearing act, leaving Jack and myself to get on with it. We left the spare boat against the towpath opposite the Griff arm while we took our butty into the basin, and then picked up the spare again to make our way to Glascote. It was dark by now, so having delivered it Jack told me to go back on the bus. I caught a late evening Midland Red en route for Coventry, and the conductor put me off near Griff; the village was some way from the main road, but I could see the lights below me.

A voice came out of the darkness as I approached the boats:

'I've med the fire up for you.' It was Bessie, who was tied up close by. I called my thanks back to Alf, and once in the cabin set about making a pot of tea.

A while later came that familiar 'pop-pop'; a slight bump, and silence.

'Noice foire' Jack announced as he entered the cabin.

'Ah' said I, 'Alf made it up.'

'Noice on 'im – any tea?'

'Ah – just mashed.'

Then it was supper, and time to turn in.

By now winter was approaching, and one Saturday found us at

Brentford waiting to load steel. We were stuck until the Monday, which left us some spare time – across the road stood a pub, and so Jack, Jimpty and I, along with a number of other boatmen, including Alf Best and Tom and Bill Hough, and even a few lightermen, paid it a visit. In the bar was a very posh sounding chap who had obviously had a few too many, who was relating the story of a golf match he had recently played. It was pretty funny, and ever afterwards, when meeting any of the others who had been there, the cry would go up:

'Been bunkered lately?'

That evening, as usual, Jack disappeared somewhere on his own. Bessie and Jimpty were both avid football fans; Brentford were playing at home, and, goodness only knows why, I let myself be persuaded to go with them. I was tired, bored, and bloody cold!

Monday came – we loaded once again, and set off for Sampson Road.

Chapter Eleven

The Oxford Road

Jack emerged from the office at Sutton's with orders to load at Griff for Oxford Power Station. There had been a time when the two Barlow companies had a virtual monopoly on this run, but now it had been taken over by Willow Wren. As you will have gathered, my knowledge of the southern Oxford Canal stretched only from Braunston to just short of Napton locks.

After passing the junction where we had always turned off for Birmingham, we began our ascent – as with all the Oxford Canal locks, these were narrow. Above Napton lay a summit, after which we began to descend again. I now remember few of the places we passed through, but one that does stick in my memory is Steeple Claydon, on the Buckinghamshire/Oxfordshire border. I'd actually been looking out for this place – my parents' neighbours back home had told me during my early towpath wanderings that the canal passed here, where the husband's family had come from. As I recall, Claydon lock was quite close to the High Street. Other places I do remember passing through were Banbury, where we saw Joe Skinner emptying at Banbury Co-op, and then Upper Heyford and Thrupp.

I thought the south Oxford to be a very twisting sort of canal, by contrast with the northern part, much of which had been straightened in the 1820s. In fact there was only one really straight section, and that was actually the site of a former tunnel, at Fenny

Compton! One thing which gave rise to this impression of a very meandering route was ‘it’. ‘It’ appeared first on one side of us, and then on the other – at one point, ‘it’ seemed to be straight in front. The mystery was finally solved when we passed ‘it’ on the towpath side, about two hundred yards away in a field – a very large radio mast.

At Aynho there was a strange diamond-shaped lock. Despite its width, it would still only hold a single boat as the sides tapered in to the ends, forming what looked like a tiny basin. After leaving Aynho lock, we travelled a short distance on the River Cherwell before another lock put us back on the canal proper. The next lock was then kept by Sam Horne, whose son (also Sam) had been the fellow who had followed me with the Skinners that time into Leicester. Sam senior kept chickens, and would barter a few eggs in exchange for some coal with passing boaters – I imagine that both parties did quite well out of this, as there were then still a number of boats going to Oxford.

The Oxfordshire countryside at last began to give way to a more urban scene, and as we descended the final flight the evening sun was shining on the spires and halls of learning for which the city is so famous. Once we had tied up and had a wash, Jack made good use of some of Sam’s eggs, with a bit of bacon and fried bread. That might seem more like a combination suitable for breakfast, but on the boats you tended to take hot meals when and where you could. The boatmen’s wives usually did the cooking while travelling the longer pounds. After supper, we sat talking for a while before settling down, ready for the hard work ahead.

Unloading was done by barrowing – the barrows were large, heavy things with iron wheels, each holding four or five shovelfuls of large coal. We all took turns at pushing the barrows and shovelling. The payment for doing our own unloading was the same as at Home Park Mill – three pounds per boat. It was heavy and dirty work, and I couldn’t help wondering how many generations of boaters had done this same job over the years – no wonder they were such a hardy people!

Of course there had been a time when men and women on the bank worked just as hard, but with the passing of time machinery had made most of their jobs so much easier. The boaters only real concession was the internal combustion engine; with the exception of one or two places, life on the canals had not changed very much from the early days. Even with the benefit of a motor boat, a boater's life was still hard, with long hours and conditions that no trade union would have tolerated. And yet, few boat people would have wanted it any other way.

Our work at the wharf finished, it was time to move on again. Another load to Oxford followed, loading at Griff again, and then one to Croxley; I was certainly glad to be working on the Junction again! For a while we were back on the steel runs to Sampson Road, with the almost obligatory coal southwards. More and more now, Jack was leaving me to steer the Bittern, even through the tunnels, something only Skipper in the past had let me do.

After a time, we resumed carrying timber to Tipton on two or three occasions, and then some empty boating. Jack didn't get so well paid for this of course, but at least we were still able to have regular meals. At last the work began to pick up again, and with it came a different cargo – baked beans, from Southall to Birmingham.

Chapter Twelve

Junction Boating Again

Over the next few months our working was pretty much confined to the Grand Union, with regular working to Birmingham with steel and the occasional load of timber. Of course this entailed running on the stretch of the northern Oxford from Braunston to Napton, and often down the bottom road to load around the Warwickshire coalfields, but mostly our trips meant using that stretch of the Grand Union between Brentford and Braunston.

Whereas the route from Napton to Birmingham was made up of flights of locks with longish pounds in between, the old Grand Junction had quite a number of individual locks separated by short pounds, especially south of Linslade. This meant there was a lot of lock-wheeling, and you would frequently meet other boaters cycling on the towpath. For pairs with only two crew members, locking this stretch could be a very tiring job, especially on a hot day.

I recall one trip when we ran into a stoppage at Marsworth. As you might expect, by the time the job was done there were quite a number of boats waiting both above and below the locks. Eventually we got moving again, but of course things were pretty chaotic; going down through Berkhamstead the towpath seemed to be crowded with lock-wheelers. Astern of our boats was Harold Collins, whose wife Clara was lock-wheeling, and ahead of us was one of her brothers, Joe Green. At one lock, Mrs Green offered me a cup of tea, and I have never been so grateful for the taste of boatman's tea in my life! However, as boats began to stop off at various places the road began to thin out until we seemed to be almost on our own. I think all three of us were relieved to get to Croxley.

Luckily it wasn't always thus. Often we would meet several pairs of boats in the day, which made life a lot easier; in those days gates were left open and paddles up, so it was just a case of straight in, and out again with little trouble. Of course the Junction journeys were a two-way thing, even if boats were only on coal runs. The Ovaltines had perhaps the fewest locks to go through, seventy in all with their last one down and first one up at Kings Langley. Boats running in and out of Brentford had to go through all hundred and two each way.

But in spite of this I think I preferred the junction out of all the parts of the Grand Union which I travelled. The big locks of the Brummagem road were quick to empty and fill, but still very hard work; I had often wondered why conventional paddle-gear wasn't used. The Leicester section wasn't too bad, except for those dratted bridges at the narrow locks of Watford and Foxton; the wide locks towards Leicester were the same as on the Junction.

I worked through another winter with Jack and Jimpty, and although for a lot of that time we carried steel there was the odd trip with timber to Tipton. Some pairs took timber to Leicester, but we never got on that run – I think it may have been British Waterways who had that contract. And as I mentioned at the end of the last chapter, Willow Wren had also obtained a contract from Heinz to carry their famous baked beans from the factory on the Paddington Arm to Birmingham.

The winter days soon passed, and it was pleasant to see the changing countryside and the leaves coming out in the hedgerows along the towpath. Spring was on its way, with the inevitable stoppages, but in the meantime we carried on, thankful that for a while there would be no more icy ropes, slippery locksides or frozen hands; soon, summer would be upon us.

We had loaded at Griff for Nestlé's one day, and on arrival at Hawkesbury were informed by the toll-clerk that there was to be a stoppage at Marsworth. It was the Tuesday before Easter – being by then late in the day, we decided to tie up at Tusses Bridge. Jack was one of Willow Wren's early captains, and was highly regarded by the company; he had been asked to pick up a film crew at Cowroast Lock and take them as far as Boxmoor. They were from the Walt Disney company, making a film about Britain for American Television.

'Well' Jack said, 'we shall 'ave to get above Maffers afore the stoppage or else we shan't get our film crew.'

'O'ny one thing to do then, ain't there' said Jimpty, 'an' that's to get a bloody move on!'

'Foive!' Jack said. I tumbled out of bed and struggled into my clothes, then set about making a pot of tea. Breakfast would be had whenever it was possible – in fact, I didn't get mine until we were above Hillmorton. Jack was already in the engine-hole when a bleary-eyed Jimpty appeared:

'Any tea?' he asked, and then added 'I'm stairved!'

The Bolinder throbbed into life and I took the tiller while Jack climbed back onto the butty, no doubt to get breakfast for Jimpty and himself.

It was a dull morning, with mist laying over the cut as it usually does over and around water. As we passed near Brinklow, a huge shadowy shape roared by, almost drowning out the sound of Bittern's engine – an express passenger train on its way to Euston Station. Suddenly the mist started to lift, and by the time we reached Hillmorton it had become a beautiful day with the sun shining on the water. The locks were soon left behind, and Jimpty took over while Jack got my breakfast; afterwards, I took the butty tiller while he tidied the cabin and mopped the boat off.

Above Braunston we met two or three pairs going to Birmingham. Jack took the motor as far as Buckby where more boats, mostly empties, were coming up, saving us the effort of lock-wheeling – several of them were Barlows, both Limited and 'Essies'. Once below the locks I took charge of the Bittern again, and continued right down to Cosgrove Lock. Albert Wilson, Ernie's brother and a former Barlow man himself, was now living in the lock cottage; he was in his garden as we drew past:

'You're in a 'urry, Jack!' Albert said.

'Ah! We'm goin' to the cocoa.' Nestlé's factory was always known as 'the cocoa'. 'We'll likely stop at Finny.'

'Soom bloody hopes' Jimpty muttered.

Once on the Fenny pound the night began to close in, and it was dark by the time we passed Great Linford. The Fenny pound in those days was largely rural, except for the town of Wolverton; lights could be seen from Newport Pagnell, or distant farms – the concrete jungle of Milton Keynes was still far in the future.

Jimpty's "some hopes" proved correct – we finally stopped at the next lock, Talbots. The lock was already drawn off, so next morning all we had to do was pull the boats in and close the gates behind us – the top gates were leaking quite a bit, so all I did was to raise the two ground paddles while Jack started the engine. I'm not sure what time we left Talbot's – I know the run to Hammond Three was about twenty minutes, and then from the top to Leighton about fifty, with loaded boats. South of Linslade, we saw a friend of mine crossing the old Black Bridge on his way to work – and he started at seven-thirty! The Black Bridge used to carry the Leighton to Luton and Dunstable railway line, until Dr Beeching stepped in, and a lot of people used it use it as a short-cut over the canal.

The film crew were waiting for us when we reached Cowroast. After the boats had entered the lock in the usual way, the fellow in charge asked Jack to reverse out with the breasted boats and go in again to let the cameraman get a better shot.

''E loves that; 'e romances' Jimpty muttered – but with Jack's prowess with the boats, who could blame him for a touch of egotism?

I had a bit of an altercation with the chief – he asked me not to look at the camera, which they'd placed on Bittern's fore-end. I retaliated by telling him that as I was raising the paddles I had to keep an eye on the level of water in the lock so that I knew when to open the gates, which put smart-alec in his place! They stayed with us to Boxmoor Lock as arranged – going down the new 'uns, Jimpty remarked:

'Thank God them booggers 'ave gone!' A sentiment I heartily agreed with.

I got away without any lock-wheeling for quite a time as a lot of boats, both loaded and empty, were coming up, intent on clearing Marsworth before the stoppage, which was to begin at six o'clock that evening. Below Croxley the sun was beginning to turn red, but it wasn't until we got to Uxbridge that darkness fell. At Cowley we stopped for a break:

'Breast up Fred' said Jack, 'I reckon we'm airned ourselves a pint.' After tying up below the lock we adjourned to a local hostelry. What a sight we must have looked among all the people who had dressed up to go out for a drink, in our overalls and donkey jackets! The place was crowded, but we managed to find ourselves a seat.

Having slaked our thirsts, we set off again along the Cowley pound, there being a good distance still to go. Jimpty and I took turns on the butty tiller, until at last we arrived and tied up. There's quite a knack to tying up a pair of loaded boats – you slow the motor, and allow the butty to run up alongside, nearest the bank. A crew member on the butty's fore-end takes up the rope from the motor's, passes it round the t-stud and ties it off with a half-hitch, while at the other end the two steerers secure the sterns together. Then someone jumps onto the bank from each end with the mooring ropes, passes them through the iron rings and ties them securely on the boats. When the boats are secured the engine is stopped, and the engine-hole doors, kept open during the day for ventilation, are closed.

Once tied up, it was time for a quick wash and then supper. After two such long days, during which we'd come from the northern-most point of the Oxford Canal to two-thirds of the way down the Junction, we were ready for our beds, and thanking the Lord that the next day was Good Friday! The next morning we got on with the domestic chores – Jack and Jimpty each cleaned one of the cabins while I mopped the boats down from stem to stern. Brasses inside and out were polished: The horse-brasses hanging by the table-cupboard, the drying rail above the stove, and the fiddle-rails actually on the stove top – these were there to prevent the kettle or pans from falling off while the boats were on the move. Then the brass chimney rings, and the tiller bar which was kept inside the motor cabin when not in use; the brass rims of the portholes, and the smaller ones on the pigeon box.

'Shan't empt afore Tuesday' said Jack: 'Yer might as well go up ter Leighton for the 'oliday.'

I put on my smart 'uniform' and a jacket, and made my way to Hayes railway station for a train to Paddington, from where I went on to Euston for the train home. But there I got a surprise – I ran into my eldest brother and sister-in-law, with their young daughter. They had been visiting her folks in London.

'Wherever have you sprung from?' my brother asked as we boarded the train; I told him our boats were at Hayes. In those days only express passenger trains had corridors – the suburban trains had compartments which would seat twelve people, and on the compartment walls there used to be pictures of the trains and countryside on the line from Euston. One of the pictures in our compartment showed a London & North-Western express passing Brinklow, with a horse-drawn narrowboat travelling south. My brother commented:

'I suppose you know that place well?'

'Yes – we passed there about five-thirty on Wednesday morning!' I replied.

We decided to have a taxi from Leighton station, as both their house and my parents' were in the same road, at the far side of town.

It was good to have home-made meals, and sleep in my own bed again – but I had to be back at Hayes by the Monday evening. Tuesday morning dawned, and with it came unloading; then after tidying up it was off to Bull's Bridge for orders – another steel run to Sampson Road. Then more coal to Croxley, following which we had to return empty. On that trip, we'd got to Stoke Bruerne, waiting in the top lock for Jack who'd gone over to the Boat Inn, when I noticed a fellow on the lockside, standing close to the stern and trying to peer inside the cabin. I was in the motor's hatches, talking to Jimpty on the butty – I pretended that I hadn't seen this chap, and when Jack returned, I wound up the speed wheel, turned the tiller and threw in the clutch. A shower of water went over matey's trousers – well, would you want some stranger peering in through your front door?

I had another problem with someone on the bank, in the days when I was boating with Jack Skinner. There is a sharp inside turn just below Hammond Three Locks, where working boats need to go close to the bank as they round the bend, and some local anglers had a habit of sitting near that turn. On one occasion, lock-wheeling, I overheard one of them grumbling about "bloody barges". Right, mate, I thought – I stopped and pointed out to him:

'If there weren't any boats, you wouldn't have a bloody canal to fish in!'

A bit later, we were coming up loaded, and misery-guts was in his usual place, still moaning. So I ran Caldy just a bit closer than usual and, having slowed down, opened the throttle again – I've never seen a landing-net whipped out of the water so fast!

From Stoke Bruerne we went on to Hawkesbury, where our orders were to load at Baddesley for Nash Mills. Then it was timber for Tipton again; from Tipton to Cannock Chase, and once more to Nestlé's. Winter came and went – I managed to get home for Christmas – and spring arrived, Easter once again, with the inevitable stoppage, this time at Braunston. Whilst we were waiting there I took a stroll up to the top lock where one of the pounds had been drained; a wizened old fellow appeared from his cottage gateway and came towards me:

'Yow wi' boats?' he asked, and when I answered that I was, he clearly mistook me to be from a boating family:

'They ain't boatmen now, they jus' knock 'em along! 'Osses were best – ah well, Oi s'pose that's progress, but Oi still say 'osses were better! 'Bye chap.' And off he went. Jack laughed when I related the tale:

'You've met 'im then?' He did tell me the old fellow's name, but sad to say I no longer remember what it was.

After the stoppage we continued on our way, with several other pairs not far behind us; we met a dozen or more on the summit, who had been waiting at Buckby. More timber boating followed, and some steel – we didn't get down the Oxford again, for which I was eternally grateful!

Summer came, and with it another stoppage, this one at Buckby. Jimpty had left us at Bedworth and I had taken the boats up to Braunston – at that time, my mother had not been too well, and Jack said I could go to Leighton if I wanted. The only problem was that Jack hadn't been paid, and so I had no money for the train, but he said:

'Me an' Jimpty'll pick yer up at Leighton to save yer coomin' all the way back, it'll probably be about Wednesday.' So I set out to hitch a lift – the one I got was not what I expected! A police car stopped beside me, and one officer asked where I was going. I explained, and they were kind enough to offer me a lift as far as Fenny Stratford; from there, I walked almost to Water Eaton before a fellow who lived in Linslade stopped and took me the rest of the way.

Early Wednesday morning I was down by the lock, and spent most of the day wandering along the towpath – no sign of Jack and Jimpty. Thursday the same, until Bill Whitlock came riding ahead of his boats down the towpath, Rose and Laura Carter following with the pair.

'Aincher goin' back then?' he asked. When I told him what Jack had said, he replied:

'Won't be coomin' – Jimpty ain't coom back.' It was then that I regretted having left Jack that day.

I never saw him again, although I heard later that he'd taken up with a lady-friend and continued boating.

And Finally...

After this incident I decided I ought to look for regular work, but whilst looking around I did get to do a couple more trips. One day, below Leighton lock, Bill and Iris appeared; they now had George Beechey's old motor, the Union Jack, and Bill asked if I wanted to work with them again. I said I didn't think so, but as I had nothing else to do, and they had offered, I said I'd like to do a run with them as they were going to Home Park.

'Oi don't loike these ingins' Bill confided, 'too much bovver goin' astern!'

The Union Jack, you may recall, had a Bolinder. Most of the time on that trip, I was the motor steerer – Iris said that if I liked they would ask Mr Barlow for another motor boat so that I could work with them, but I wasn't ready to go back.

A little later I met up with Joe Bray. He was married now, and asked if I would like to give him a hand, which I was more than willing to do; they were going to Nash. After emptying there, it was down to Bull's Bridge for orders – seeing the old place again, I was very tempted. Joe's orders were to load wheat at Brentford for Toovey's Mill, just above Langley Lock, but they were going to be there over the weekend, so I thought it was best if I made my way back home. A few weeks later I obtained work as a lorry driver with a brick company, and it appeared that my days as a dry land sailor were over.

Although it was just a short period in my life, I would not have missed it for anything. I still have fond memories of the people I met, who so willingly took me into their world – many of them, sadly, have now passed away: Bill Humphries, Jack Wilson, Jack Munk, his nephew Henry, Joe Bray, "Skipper" John Knill, Joe and Rose Skinner, Bill and Rose Whitlock, and others whose passing I haven't heard about.

The canals and those who worked on them, both on the boats and on the bank, contributed much to the wealth of this country. If we ever get a government sufficiently far-sighted, perhaps they will again one day, and the working narrowboat will become as familiar a sight to new generations as it was to mine and those before. We can always hope!

Frederick R. Hobbs
Linslade, 2002

Appendix I

About the Boats

I expect that many of you who have picked up this book will be familiar with the type of boat that I was working on in those distant days, but for any who are not so sure, I thought that maybe I should write a little about them.

My days on the cut were spent on working narrowboats. The design of the narrowboat was originally dictated by the dimensions of the early canals – the technology of the time meant that the first locks were only large enough to handle a boat that was seventy feet long and seven feet wide, and this remained the size of the 'standard' working boat through to the end of canal carrying. There were some minor variations – the new fleet of boats built in the 1930s for the Grand Union Canal Carrying Company were actually 71' 6" long, which the company had determined as the maximum possible size which would pass through the locks on the Birmingham Canal Navigations. Around the Black Country, in the latter days trains of joey boats would be hauled by tugs, which were basically just a big engine in a short hull – these tended to be between forty and sixty feet long, while the joeys were the usual seventy.

And some special boats were built to work solely on the Wolverhampton level, a continuous pound of over twenty miles from the top of Wolverhampton locks to central Birmingham and

Gas Street Basin – the so-called 'Hampton Boats' were eighty feet long.

Other types of boat were used on the southern waterways:

Both FMC and the GUCCCo experimented with wide boats, built to resemble a narrowboat with living cabins but ten feet wide, intended to run from London to Birmingham through the widened locks of the Grand Union route. A good idea which failed because the last of the locks (at Camp Hill) were never widened; and the difficulty of working through the tunnels, meeting other boats, was never resolved.

Joey boats, which I mentioned above, were used for short-distance work around Birmingham – they were crude and lightly-built, mostly with no cabin although a few had little day-cabins for brewing tea and eating the 'snap'. Most were double-ended – the rudder and towing mast could be moved from one end to the other, saving the effort of having to turn the boat around.

Barges, mostly horse-drawn, were used sometimes on the lower end of the Grand Junction where the channel allowed, up as far as Berkhamstead. Most had cabin accommodation; the hulls were 71' by 13'

Lighters were used around the docks and to transfer cargoes to and from Brentford Basin. Unpowered, with no accommodation, they were twelve feet wide, and pulled by horses or tugs.

To come back to the narrowboats: There were two basic variations, the motor boat and the butty, which was the unpowered 'trailer', if I can use lorry terms. The butty boats were exactly the same as the early horse-drawn boats – the design of a towed vessel had been refined over 150 years and was just as suited to being towed by a motor-boat as by a horse. The fore-ends were pretty much identical (boaters never refer to the 'bow'), but the butty stern tapered elegantly from below the cabin, upswept to a huge wooden rudder which was hung on two large hooks. The upper part was known as the Ram's Head, into a square hole in which was fitted the heavy curved wooden tiller – in boating terms, the whole assemblage would be referred to as the 'Ellum (helm). The tiller could be reversed – in use, it curved down to swing just above the cabin roof at a comfortable height, and when tied up it was turned the other way up to curve upwards, out of the way of people entering or leaving the cabin.

The motor's stern, by contrast, came to a semi-circular shape known as the counter. Below the waterline, the hull tapered in beneath the counter, and the propeller was set underneath with the metal rudder swinging from a vertical shaft which passed through the counter behind it. The top of the rudder post had an s-shaped steel bar attached which brought the tiller to a comfortable height, and a detachable tubular tiller slipped onto this, usually with a wooden handle fitted. The tiller itself was removed and kept inside the cabin when tied up, again to allow easier access to and from the cabin. The counter deck was flat, whereas the butty stern had a recessed well set into it – a cupboard at the back of that well was the boatman's equivalent of a 'fridge! Set against the outside of the hull, and usually below the waterline, it could be relied upon to stay nice and cool, and so ideal for keeping things fresh, like the marble slab in an old-fashioned pantry.

The motor's cabin is quite a bit taller than that on the butty. The headroom inside (or lack of it!) is the same, but the propeller shaft passes beneath the cabin on the motor, meaning that the whole thing must be set higher in the hull. And from the outside, the motor cabin appears much longer – but the front few feet are actually the engine-room (or engine-'ole, to a boater!). The big diesel engines first used in boats, like the Bolinder, needed a lot of space to accommodate them, and their need for regular attention necessitated plenty of room around them, as well. The interior of all the cabins are built to the same basic design, even if there are tiny variations between boats from different builders. Inside, the cabin is around eight feet long and not much over six feet wide; the sides taper in slightly below the gunwale, and rather more so above, as the cabin has a degree of tumble-home to allow it to clear the arch of bridge-holes. After the canal-boats act of 1877, this space was only (!) allowed to accommodate two adults and three children.

Access to the cabin is through double doors at the stern end, with a sliding hatch set in the roof above. Just inside is a step, where the steerer normally stands (safety note – never, never, never steer a motor boat standing on the counter! People have been killed when a sudden need for reverse gear has swept the tiller around and knocked them overboard and into the blades). From here, you step down onto the top of the coalbox, which sits on the floor below, and thence to the floor of the cabin. To your right, the back wall of the cabin houses small cupboards and/or shelves; below, a bench about eighteen inches wide runs along the cabin wall all the way to the front, divided about two-thirds of the way along by a cutaway bulkhead, often with a hinged flap.

The rear part of this is the side-bed, where one or two children would sleep at night whilst it was used for seating during the day; underneath is a clothes drawer or maybe a cupboard. The front part of the cabin, beyond the bulkhead, is the bed-hole where mum and dad sleep. More drawers are fitted below the right-hand part, the continuation of the bench, with a clear space above and on some boats a porthole in the cabinside; to the left, a cupboard reaches from floor to ceiling, with drawers below and shelves above a central part which drops down at night, meeting the bench to form the cross-bed. The grown-ups sleep with their feet inside the cupboard!

In the rear of the cabin, to the left, is the range, set on its own sturdy shelf. Coal-burning, it is a smaller version of what you might still find in a country house kitchen, with removable hot-plates and a small oven. Hanging next to it is the handbowl, a circular metal bowl with a tubular handle which serves as washing-up bowl and hand-basin; soap and cloths live in tiny recesses in the adjacent back wall of the cabin. Between the stove and the bed-hole another floor-to-ceiling structure houses three cupboards and a narrow drawer where the cutlery is kept – the central cupboard, just above the drawer, has a round-ended door which hinges down to form a small but sturdy table. This is the table-cupboard; the drawer is often known as the crumb-drawer, because it also serves to catch crumbs when the table-cupboard is closed! Set under the cabin-top just inside the doors is another small drawer, easily accessible to the steerer – this is the ticket-drawer, where the toll-tickets and loading papers are kept to hand.

The inside of the cabin is bright, with the polished brass of the stove's fiddle-rails, the drying rails above, and often a set of old bed-knobs screwed to a board and hung inside the doors. Fancy lace-plates adorn the cabin walls above the stove, colourful painted flowers appear around the cabin and on the inside of the doors with a landscape (castle) scene on the table-cupboard door, and hand-crocheted lacework hangs below the ticket-drawer, around the opening into the bed-hole and along many of the shelf edges.

The biggest part of a working boat is of course the cargo hold. The hold of a motor boat was a few feet shorter than the butty's, because of the space taken up by the engine – that, and the weight of engine and drive-train, reduced the potential load by about five tons. The usual load for a pair was around 55 tons, 30 of them in the butty, but some cargoes filled the available space before that kind of weight was reached. On the canals, the hold was usually known as the boat's bottom, and it was notionally divided into four sections: Fore-end, back o' the mast, middle and back end. There was no actual division between these, except for a heavy wooden beam which spanned across the hold at gunwale height – the gunwale was the four/five inch wide ledge around the top edge of the hull. Below each beam, a chain also spanned the boat's hull, which could be tightened to keep the sides straight and prevent them spreading under a loose load, and each beam was perforated by a slot through which a tapered vertical stand rested on the bottom of the hold and supported the top-planks above the load. The first beam was different, however – its back edge was cut away to fit around the mast, a square-section vertical box with an inner section which could be raised or lowered – the butty would often be towed by a line from the top of the mast when loaded, which some boaters led back through running-blocks to a t-stud on the cabin-top as I mentioned in my story.

At the fore-end, a triangular deck with a hatch set in it covered an enclosed storage space for spare ropes and the like, with a solid bulkhead behind it. Above this bulkhead, a wooden board was normally fitted, triangular but with a cut-off flat top about a foot wide. From this deck-board the first top-plank reached back to the mast; then, another went as far as the middle stand, a third back to the next stand and a last back to the cabin-top.

On butties, with their lower cabins, this plank was often curved to come down to a wooden block set on the cabin roof. A few feet behind the deck-board there was usually an A-frame set in place, with the front cloths fixed over it – this structure and the space beneath used to keep the other cloths and assorted paraphernalia was known as the cratch – the whole thing could be taken down if necessary to clear low bridges, like the one at the entrance to Griff colliery. Wooden uprights, notched at each end, would be fitted between gunwale and top-plank between the stands to support the planks and form the triangular shape of the covering cloths.

To cover a perishable or weather-sensitive cargo, the cloths were used: Side cloths, long continuous tarpaulin sheets, were permanently attached along the gunwale each side, rolled tightly and held down with light strings when not in use. They would be unrolled and drawn up the sides of the structure formed by uprights and planks – long strings attached to one side cloth would reach over the planks, through eyelets in the other cloth, and then tie off at the planks to hold them in place. Then the top cloths, in four sections roughly matching the sections of the hold, were laid over them, along the planks and reaching almost down to the gunwale again so that there was a big overlap to keep the rain out! More strings clipped to rings along the gunwale to reach over the top to the other gunwale, through the rings the other side and again back to tie off at the top, holding them in place.

Running empty, the side cloths would be rolled up, the top cloths folded carefully and stored under the cratch or in the fore-end locker; if the cratch was left up, as many boaters did, the front part of the side-cloth remained raised, its edge tapering down to the roll along the gunwale from there back, and a special short cloth used in place of the full top cloth. The strings on this permanent part of the cloths were always scrubbed to a brilliant white, and tied in a very ornamental fashion, such was the pride of the boaters in their turn-out.

I hope this brief description will help anyone who doesn't know them to have an idea of how the boats looked. There are a good number of these old boats still around the canals today, and the best suggestion I can make is to go and take a look for yourselves!

Appendix II

Working the Boats

I'm sure also that most of you who are sufficiently interested to be reading my book will have some experience of handling boats on the canals in the modern, leisure era, so you'll have a good idea of what is entailed in going through locks. But at the same time, the art of working a pair through in the days when time was money, and the pressure was on the captain and crew to 'get 'em ahead', is quickly fading from the waterways of today. So I hope the following will give you a feel of what it was like!

Imagine if you will that you are the captain of a pair of loaded boats, steering the motor along the Grand Junction and approaching a lock from below. Hopefully, the lock will be ready for you – either set by your own lock-wheeler or, if you are lucky, left ready by a pair going the other way. In the days of trade, locks were always left with the gates open and the paddles up upon leaving, so that is how you find your next lock. Two boat's lengths (remember the boat is seventy feet long) from the lock you slow down, the towrope slackens so you coil it in as the butty catches you up; then as your fore-end passes the bottom gates you put the engine astern, also holding the tiller so that it doesn't swing around and give you a nasty bruise. It could even knock you off into the water!

As the butty's fore-end passes you, you drop the towrope onto its fore-deck having taken it off of the motor's dolly, and then put the engine back into forward gear and drift up to the cill of the lock, a kind of door-step below the top gates. The forward drive keeps the boat against the cill as you climb onto the cabin-top and heave yourself up onto the lockside – no lock-ladders then! – and close the gate behind you and drop the paddle.

Alongside, the butty steerer runs his boat in beside the motor and removes the tiller, lying it on the cabin-top so that it cannot catch the lock-wall. He (or she, of course) steps off onto the steps beside the bottom gate as the butty drifts on into the lock with the long heavy strap in his hand, takes it up and throws it over the balance beam and around the paddle-post on the gate and then around the first bollard on the lockside, thus using it to brake the boat to a halt against the cill. Once stopped, the strap then goes just around the bollard alone, and the steerer closes that gate and drops the paddle.

You both then go to the top end of the lock and raise the paddles – ground paddles first, of course, then the gate paddles, usually known as 'centres' to the boaters. With the lock full, the butty steerer coils the strap and places it back neatly on his cabin-top. The motor steerer runs the boat forward, picks up the towrope and drops it back over the dolly on the stern. A slight run astern to slow the boat and prevent the tow breaking as it takes up the strain, and then you are away out of the lock.

Going downhill, the procedure was much the same except that the motor would be left out of gear, the flow of water through the bottom paddles keeping the boat against the bottom gates and so clear of the cill as it descended. The butty would not be tied to the bollard, but a line from the stern taken in a loop over the centre paddle spindle – this would be used by the steerer from within the stern well to draw the butty back against the cill when the lock was empty, allowing the space for the bottom gates to swing into the lock-chamber.

With the gates open, the motor steerer would jump down onto his boat and set it in motion, taking up the tow as before. If you were two-handed, one man could open both gates by 'stepping', shoving the butty's gate open with his foot while standing on the end of his own gate and then pushing that open with the balance beam.

With empty boats, things were often a lot simpler. Empty pairs would usually run breasted-up on much of the Junction, for example from Bull's Bridge down to Brentford to load, or even from the mills at Apsley, Croxley, Frogmoor and elsewhere. Coal-boats returning empty, as Barlows frequently did, to the coal-fields would run breasted all the way to Cowroast Lock, meaning that the pair needed only one steerer. But narrow locks, like the Oxford and Coventry Canals, or on the BCN, meant working each boat through separately, effectively doubling the amount of work.

If you had other boats travelling in front of you, the locks would be set against you as you approached. This is where the lock-wheeler came in – one member of the crew would cycle ahead and set each lock before the boats got there. He would then stay to help until the lock was filling (or emptying) and then cycle on again to the next. If he saw other boats approaching, he would turn back, signalling to his crew that someone was coming the other way.

A good, efficient crew could whistle through locks in a time that seems impossible today – if some of the day's travels I have described in the book seem incredible, that was how it was done!

More titles from this publisher overleaf...

'A beautiful tale, beautifully told... this has got to be a winner.'

Roger Wickham, Amherst Publishing

Departing from the detective novels for which he is known, in *Starlight* Geoffrey Lewis tells a tale of schoolboy friendship set against the backdrop of the Oxford Canal in the days when the commercial trade was in decline; the canal itself threatened with closure. In a story where the mood ranges from heartwarming humour to unbearable poignancy, he conjures up the world of the 1950s; factual events and real characters flit past in the background as he leads the reader through the long heat-wave of the summer of 1955, as it was seen by an eleven-year-old boy living in a little North Oxfordshire village.

Starlight was published in 2005 – for more information, please check our website at www.sgmpublishing.co.uk.

ISBN 978-0-9545624-5-8. Cover price £6.99.

'So accurate is the content, we recommend these books to our trainee crews.'

Nick Wolfe, The Narrowboat Trust

With the publication of *The New Number One* in March 2009, the Michael Baker trilogy is complete.

It all started when ten-year-old Michael Thompson had had enough. Mentally and physically abused by his drunken father, treated like a skivvy by his mother, he had taken all that his miserable life could throw at him; but then the final blow came when his dog was taken away as well: On a bitter cold night in January, 1940, he set out to commit suicide – but all does not go according to plan…

The three books tell a story of England's canals through the Second World War and beyond. The pressure and the pain, the humour and resilience of the boating people. Tragic and heart-warming, this trilogy charts the progress of a job becoming ever more difficult, against the broader panorama of worldwide events.

'Northamptonshire's own answer to Inspector Morse'

Image Magazine

'Impossible to put down'

ChoiceMagazine

'Plots brimming with unexpected twists'

What's On Magazine

These four D.I. David Russell novels may be ordered from any good bookshop.

'If you like crime novels, I thoroughly recommend these – and if you don't, read them anyway, you might be converted.'

Glen Peckett, Endeavour

Flashback by Geoffrey Lewis	ISBN 978-0-9545624-0-3
Strangers by Geoffrey Lewis	ISBN 978-0-9545624-1-0
Winter's Tale by Geoffrey Lewis	ISBN 978-0-9545624-2-7
Cycle by Geoffrey Lewis	ISBN 978-0-9545624-3-4

published by SGM Publishing.

SGM Publishing

35 Stacey Avenue, Wolverton, Milton Keynes, Bucks MK12 5DN

info@sgmpublishing.co.uk